*as to what
would help these works find their way through the culture very little
would help books of this type find their way through culture   we
sell very few books   we generally dont participate in all of the
cultures sacred rituals or respect its values and we have a whole
set of counter positions on almost everything   and feel perhaps
not content with that   but satisfied that we are doing what we
want to do which stands like a screw in the shoe of anybody holding
a place in the dominant culture*

—David Antin

a screw in the shoe

Anthology of Challenges

Edited by Lou Rowan

Golden Handcuffs Review Publications
Seattle, Washington

Golden Handcuffs Review
Publications

Editor

Lou Rowan

Contributing Editors

David Antin
Andrea Augé
Bernard Hœpffner
Stacey Levine
Harry Mathews
Rick Moody
Toby Olson
Jerome Rothenberg
Scott Thurston
Carol Watts

LAYOUT MANAGEMENT BY PURE ENERGY PUBLISHING, SEATTLE
WWW.PUREENERGYPUB.COM

Libraries: *this is Volume II, #22.*

Information about subscriptions, donations, advertising at:
www.goldenhandcuffsreview.com

Or write to: Editor, Golden Handcuffs Review Publications
1825 NE 58th Street, Seattle, WA 98105-2440

Contents

FICTION

COLLABORATIONS

AUTOBIOGRAPHY

ESSAY

CONVENTIONAL PUBLISHING AT WORK

REVIEWS

Kiosk

Carol Watts

A border kiosk opened in the night.
In the dark, in a corner of my room.
In that district of my mind that carries
heat of tarmac and exhaust, the noise
of European tramways.

I search for my papers in another language.
That language is mine, it thickens to graffiti.
How long have I stood by while it thickens.
Always so foreign, now I house it in sleep.
Look at its hate.

I have no papers to get by. The kiosk sits
in the corner of my room and the day
is beginning, its first flush. How will I reach
the sanctity of streets. There are men smoking
there, taking a break.

Perhaps the radio will distract them while
I dress. But the kiosk has a naked electric light.

Walls are peeling in its dryness. Birds
start up outside, already on the move.
My breathing clangs.

I refuse to host this border kiosk silently
but it is rooted deep as a wart. They tell me
to wake up and find my papers if I am
to breakfast. I have no papers. They sit
between me and the door, like guns.

A border kiosk opened in the night, in the dark.
My papers are insufficient but they say they can
go by the eye. Look into the screen and all
will be well, and there will be coffee in the sun.
So day comes.

7 Poems

Andrea Brady

All My Sons

The invisible Marcus
is painting the ceiling. When we slept together
he was painting the walls
the shade of a number problem, a veil,
he lingers on the adult side where television
is not a ration and the poem is a manner
of holding it together. Do you think it's right

that only certain people can be famous?
To extend the definition and give us each
half a chance would keep us from getting ancient.
We climb elephant-coloured branches,
the air is free like us in the entire world under
a state dept. travel warning.

It's given out that a wild boar has seized a train,
the hoof prints lead to Calais.
When its blood is up it has a blind stamina

the rough edge of its hair rubs off its skin,
the skin keeps it from sliding into the hole
of a carnivorous tree into slavery,
if it is silent it will soon be laughing
burning like a herd of suns over the fields
of Fukushima.

The girl must be a Peshmerga
boar-spear or dragon, she chooses
the blue and white sail and circles indefinitely
above the Angolon. These fierce and slender limbs
climb jugs and divots, she flies
breaking nuance among the pine tops
but would be the child I lost,
her lungs scissored by an epoch
or she goes out drowned in scarlet.

The boys are also ones I would have lost,
and may yet, the pitiless front
of their jammies maps every place
that is not a target, it is the single dinosaur
who might have evolved into a man but is now
a relic they dig out of bricks for fun.
The box overhead shows a heaven made in ash.
They grow towards it forcing a trope of fear
as a thing to be managed or blamed.

I saw the heavies of special branch
in the departure lounge guarded by seven gates
and seven crowns. They chose the boys
for their ballistic look and the girls as slaves
who fell through that fabled hole in their bodies.
Waking up with a sword, smashing the wrist with trucks.
I snatch him away

he has been flipping his brother his whole body
shakes and can't be held in fear
of my outrageous discipline. He asks only for special time
riding the 38 in a loop, London's carbolic sky

full of canaries and cancer, we agree
each chapter must end with 'boobytrap'.
At night his head rests on owls.

There are only four people in this room. We
threaten to leave the table
in Vienna as a sandpit full of fox piss,
leave the children by dying off to
pick each other up under the arms,
make a catenary arch on Hatterall ridge
and subsist as best they can forever.
Their skin is still dripping; putting the head
through the hole is doubly impossible,
how can they make food or lodging?
He consoles himself picking out carbine stars
and multiplying them by larger numbers, sketching
out groups

of fish and cupcakes and imagining filling the toad.
What is the number before infinity?
What does produce mean? That the art of holding
is palliative, and no one need live
having lost her sparkle.

Tonight it's claw club, the lesson
Gothic mathematics,
each werewolf sleeps in a cubicle where in the daytime
it does some clerical work.
In combination they produce feelings
which take the place of the sum;
the tv is full of spying numbers,
they shoot out of the arm of the sofa,
the brain quivers with disco as a rubiate x marks
their zone of landing.

You are a bonkenger called rhubarb.
That means fighting but then holding
hands with strangers at soft play,
crying when asked to be sorry as if

your entire personality was on the spit
at the despatch
box. The fox
fought with the breakfast till it turned into dinosaurs
and was cleared away.
We water-board amoxicillin,
owning the good we claw back his shut face.
To make up that good with sweet
night gardens believing
we are rescuing their ears. The analyst
saw this child

as an artist whom the mother records
shouts into oblivion
wishes to repair sometimes
like a clock whose singular complexity she keeps,
is shoved off, anxiously needed.
But he recoiled from being fed on too.
Retreated into the hollow trunk of a tree
where none could command him to communicate,
a prince of lost countries.

Smiling over the field
of poppies like a good witch their mothers
feed them with their own images
which is the lie of their harmlessness,
which puts them to sleep
instead of killing them.

That is a strong place. Like Socrates
the baby tied to his pushchair waits
in his bedroom with a blanket covering his head
for death; the child drifting in and out of reality
in his bedroom
with pythons and rats,
his wrists held by wires
to the fire-guard, and nothing will save him.
The sky bulges with giant bullets,

but only an individual retches bringing
nothing up but the desire to know nothing again.

I must get back to my own.
The only consolation
of mornings like this one is that their damage
can be so easily held.

Day Song

What is the value of this number? It hangs in the air
remote as bells, it swings in the sheer air
is up. The dog blundering in heliotrope

as a colour lives a fast stupid way,
which burns through too fast for thought,
and so is gone again

to whatever house picks the snow.
Contrails scratch its glass
but the curls also dry

as the flesh-eating sun does its tricks
glider slips downwards on a blade of grass
becoming natural through this fearless

collapse in the vast abstraction of sky.
Poster girls all have open mouths
our archives a vast emptiness of money

and squandered protection which apes
the thicknesses of all historic thought,
or possibly only this film of liquid creeping vividly

along the floor. The field of offerings is perfect
streaming a number which is zero's oddness
even making that sky blue.

What I thought was a face is a metal plate
this is not an arbitrary proposition
unlinked to the others, like the collective,

films of lives no one wants
keep us sad in the evening, or crammed with gore,
working out our psychotic wishes in that gap

between the subject and its community,
object, master, the police. I can fight with you
only if I believe you are immortal, like every day

comes a different way up the track
or falls like thunder out of the sky
and floods the screen I send this to.

Insomniad New

The bird door, billows
behind which a pinked sky bulges
with fluff and dirigibles, every one
opened and shapeless like the new
school where I take the kids,
her kids, but they are mine,
out under showers to the country,
away from the other mother's
neglect, packing their summer clothes,
but what about my job, the waiter
with his canapés hesitates then nodded.

The country from above
is velvet peaks, the grass golden
and soft as icing, the trees wine-
dark though in New England pink
to gold. I weep here, by the boards,
the grass is long the ringing
of the hardball chucked in my face
subsides into our possible life;

sinking and hooking
back up above the icy surface,
fevers curdle in my armpits, my mind
knotted in a hideous pink bow,
then it simplifies like a triumphal arch.
The line needs no defence
and is endlessly reformed:
does your mother know you're here?

Stridor

She thins the rib skin leaping clavicle,
her life in the summer bed always full
of sand is a boring thoracic effort,
her pelt luminous as mayonnaise.

From the park lofts Pharrell Williams
the summer disguised as Lollards
and the children too weak for pitching
still sleep with basilisks and etch on dawn

with their porous bones. Still sleep
covered with the mama dog,
contactable by dirty men.
I say so because I never know

when I may need to, the synthetic
crepes twist spagyrically on the washing lines
made of an obligation rather than an intensity.
And the wild boar took out my liver, she said,
and used it as a flag. Actually

it was someone else's liver. I knew by its
mushroom birthmark, stretching
as the leg grew out of its cast. The crossers
made little headway with their bat-and-ball
lollies, licking them like cats, but the others

were leaning away from animals
and the doctors knew they were wrong
by the way they barked all day
they sweated into the night.

Salthouse

You are softness   suspended
in the edgy air,   oh corporal
of selection   noises.   And you touch
the dust makes patterns   in creases,
whorled and deep   and heavy as a nautilus.
Succeeded by your others   illuminators
creationists paled and flattened   by the need
for sleep, we watch them   mistake
midnight's cockerel and   shoe
the snake in hooves.   They watch us
like white wolves   cattish and   healthy
in trees.   In the depth   which is still
our lives, own, we   melt   and frost
making our centre   a certaine
knot of peace.   These limbs   your reach
harden and rooted   in elective ground,
the fathoms vibrate with monsters   overwhelmed
push yourself up from the dive   you are now
running with melted sugar   and close
your primitive organs,   dry yourself
and take back yourself   across that broken bridge.

S / L E D G E S

The possibility of life in the mind
of you living on such a brink table
top, ice of the Gospel giving
out tickets to hunters of wild angels

or furriers blazing search in gorse
for mice, hardly in winter, ticking
over of engines and popping warms
honey-coloured blood with sparks

from their halos or the circuit held in place
in barrel-chested batteries like treacle.
To see you all gripped by fire
and to see a summer walk

round the Ewyas with sky for
a canopy are two indefinite futures,
the catastrophe eliminates any
indifferent particles, hunters

turn back in deference from the high
flattened roadworks and you take
leisure to turn your face up
towards buzzards or were finches in

hail. The infant cupped in his cradle
seat, one of three kings illuminating
the pass with their gifts of horse,
shit and chocolate, and firs

blow out a melody of snowflakes
to the white queen of their inscrutable
origin their downloadable patterns
their weight in multitudes and fine singularity.

We turn back rudely, hastily, too near
peaks to risk annoying our company
too far from loneliness to see snow
perish under a hot mystic tread. At home

with pies we recreate satisfaction.
The wind like a lake bears
steadily down on the house, luckily
it's got thick medieval walls

the walls are still standing. Let the pouring
beat up the fields, let it defeat sheep
and gobble the grass. Let ancient minstrels
serenade the pederasts among the cultivated

skin laid flat as the history of this valley.
We have as much to keep as an infinite
hayrick, it glows with honey-
coloured potency, we should work hard

to keep it all alive and ready to wander
the night if our care does more
than teach their gross needs to blow
outwards we must keep hold of them

firing the night with their sainted hearts
as we banish death with dreams
and the miraculous novelties
incarnated as love himself.

The light pulls off.
The light fades into
sound, so sounding spits and becomes
flat and wide: light salts,
whose angles hurt,
dumb windows break
letting in the whole sea.
The sea heaves. It pushes
the sound gets in everywhere
first and is a coiling sensation.
The hand breaks. The hand is flat
under the roller, the sea
does everything it intended.
The hand is transparent
so thin as held rice. Light pushes
through it onto the ant face.
The ant face has two lines for eyes.
A sound insults the eyes

behind the lines like a garlic press
and the night sits not
vomited in the stomach
with the meal paid. The meal
is ground and scattered
behind the eye where the people
and the objects skitter
against the flap which holds them
cannot hold them still. The cars roar
as the light begins and the reasons
crawl through the see-
through hand with the bird
singing out frère Jacques has no use.
The sound of roaring shuts
behind creaking roses
standing at the security desk
an apology: rose salt
cusses the Christmas turkey,
her excess skin tucked back against her
hole shamefully, where the slaughterman
falters. The ant at home at sea
the triple barrel of the sea in museum
windows, presses light
out of the language
interfering with children
whose salted angles spit
a normal sound,
a little light music in pots,
a little hungover tremble that beats
its coiled vapour against the sea.
The spring creaks, a ring
pounds hatefully on its coil
when the eggs break
out in spots, turned on
a high-voltage lamp to check
the specimen grows.
The face turns and creaks
towards the door the smell of fat
of trickles and bad tenancies.

The press creaks. The light
is the last layer before the painting,
it holds up its sainthood to the sea,
the sea spits and roars in shameless
security at the wake
up, and roll
over into the light. The day spits.
The roses twist into the shaft,
the yellow crop spreads poisonously
in fen light for meal.
The breach appeals. The balls split
off from the head sing out
Mary had a little lamb so they are not
split off at all as the whole is,
the new line rolls out. Rolling out
of sound go the ant-tracks
under the whole sea. The sea burns.
It doesn't give. It doesn't give you
doesn't give a shit doesn't give away
doesn't give credit doesn't give notice
doesn't give room doesn't give credence
doesn't give thanks doesn't give refunds
doesn't give space doesn't give space
the space forgets. The energy disperses.
The matter splits the head splits like
wise is wrapped in tissue in the bin.
The tissues are counted and some are whole.
The light spoils. The light spreads out
the meat spoils, it hangs in the cooler
and as the muscle relaxes the taste
of the hole becomes more
nuanced, the slash
in the eye marks a line ending
as a row ploughed or turned
is salted by the eye breaking
itself on its field. The field so cranked
and normal is imputed to that hate
tucked into the roses like a flap of skin
so obviously it shudders there

in the engine's place. The roller
continues flattening the road.
The sea and its weight
continue in the place of the light
which constricts to the size needed
for a fly
on the wall incinerator, the pill
is placed carefully on the paper hand,
the light splits and either side of the light
is bleached with the inflation that sticks
in the pill which sticks in the throat,
the multiples shoot out
of the pill is a fly dangling in water
but it is not fake. The choice is not fake
the choice is fake the light is fake
the sound is not fake, as it grates the eye
and the light is fake, it fades,
it pulls off
a little trick, the museum shuts,
the sea shuts, the holes shut,
the children shut, the sky corrodes
where the breach dangles its pealed
edible drop of fat skin and the sound
giggles the hand
slips out of its envelope
where it has its reasons the reasons burn.
The reasons burn as the pill takes
and the bicep coils around its flimsy origin,
flimsy right, the right to light
scalded against the things, the dust. The inventory.
The fronds drip into the bowl
they count as an inventory, even the one
holding its secret original poultry,
the split between what is done for or to
a wall of muscle splitting the sea
and the salt in the cistern is there for good reason.
The heaviness of water which eyes must lift
if they will look out
will look out for others

will look out for you
will look out for the slaughterman
will look out for saints
will look out for rollers
will look out for fowl
will look out for reasons
will look out for refunds
will look out for breaks
through a line, a salt, a spit
sliced through its skin
to see
if it runs
clear.

Print

Maurice Scully

Might be the 10th.
Early spring.
Quarter past
six. Dark.

The action of
burning's a
complex action.
Crumpled

paper napkin
with a base
pattern of
indentations

overlaid with
a pattern of
pumpkins

mushrooms
peppers
their names
in clear letters

under circular
stains where a
cup was placed –
the action of

fending for yrself.
A pencil over a
printer's
ear.

Narrow
floorboards fit
snug & shining
to the door.

One foot
on the ground,
two.

The most energetic
rays which reach
the earth's surface are
those to which

our eyes respond
& which we
call 'light'.
Right.

To prefer plants
to tar. Just
that.

Catherine tugged
playfully at the large
zipper & was
astonished at how

easily & fluidly.
The rain beat a
little tattoo on the
window. A siren

far away in the
city added. Warm.
Already. She had
not followed the

sequence. Jack
shivered. The moon?
He was taken
aback.

To begin
again, the whisper
of the pen on
the page.

Well I don't know
tangles sparks
crumpled up tellings
a "mental refuge

from the realities
of life" – all that.
Hug tight the
comforting falsities

or take the blunt
actual to heart – your
choice. Tiny florets
on a wall-top

a passing crow
staining the pathway
ahead with a crisp
click white.

3 Poems

John James

Studio Poem

for Bruce & Rosy McLean

how to compare the incomparable
allora where does this interior light
stem from it illuminates
vast planes of the canvas
carrying some sort of assured calm
in broad & apparently random brush strokes
paler than cyan making a space
that acts on the heart like a balm

now is the moment to draw
some lines on the white A4
the writer is slow but the page is patient
having no hesitation
in leaving a few notes out
like Ashkenazy

Romsey, Take 2

the prions are in everything now
including the flies that you eat
as you walk down the street

but above the ridge tiles
a thrush is chanting
those who love have hope to bring

the slate is not so dark
though beauties you have few
but cherish those you do

it's Saturday & the Bohemian proletariat
gather at The Empress at six thirty sharp
the talk is of a Portuguese departure

as the blackbird sings
Virilio Virilio

Vocalise

*Ich leb' allein in meinem Himmel
in meinem Lieben, in meinem Lied!*
                    -- Friedrich Rückert

from cutting shapes
clouds disappear

it's 6:45 p.m.
at La Manière

a sip of Fontcaude
before dinner

the stars will soon arrive
above the courtyard

beneath their gaze
take a pill for pollen

it'll be a
long long time

before the night's
over tonight

& two logs
don't make a light

Two Poems

Sarah Hayden

from *Sitevisit*

the stripes surveille as flat she sleeps

incotton inhumed

a sphere that seals all of its mysteries inside

a ball all gentle glowing

high away

impossible enclosure

as though it grew that way

but without the mess of sepals, the peeling and the dust &c &c

rhodoid I wonder will you ever run out

a doe: squarish and static

but lightninglit none the less

and some creatural other essence, too. a one that augurs a more welcoming embrace.

her room he calls rosâtre. she shuts her eyes at the in-sanguination.

mornings: delvaux like, she moves about, pondering 'pon the wa(i)st(e) of her

nights: lies untwisting, or arranges limbs in momentary geometries of unweighed relief

an early request for a door was ill made & ill received. she invests in them a supernal authority, soothing & fuguing, it

makes solid the stripes.

<call me when your velovent is installed>

Prodding the softening rims of
ambivalence,
a class debates the ethics of anyone in a
jacket so silver determining the quotidian
of a mass variegate as this. Holding a Neu!
Neu! Romantic Sublime in one hand, and
palpating the tried eyelids and calves of
an historic alien colony in the other, they
are [queasy]

They are
feeling their affiliations with certain
typefaces, sugarcubes, oversaturated
reproduction///
                                    rub and snag against
            the unignorability of that shuttling stench

i like how my house is high
not alone the eeyrie-existence of our fourteenth floor
but the raisedup beginnings of it.
an iron lady who plucks at petticoats to show her ankles: four square

under her skirts
snow is inclined to linger
when all the rest has all melted, all clean & away
it shines there// sounding a unitone
advertizing its hiding place as though it never wanted
anyway
to play cache-cache

she draws a grids, its segments clear & clean

eraser tight
the other triggered fist
is ever-ready
any undesirable intermixture of functions is willed, it will, be avoided

twisting boiffard-bits sign up to as extras in an ersatz scatter piece but
the line spools intransigent.

A child who knelt to play at trains

Grown up and all away
counts the insta-shrinkage of skin
in contexts of any disturbance

oso   evenly   applied

calendular in such circumstances
is a chromatic system
extreme & intransigent

or:

through the eyes
this   viscous unguent
a   thick   layer

then:
the frantic creature stills its wings
roads are cleared
                straightened

channels open
matches are remade

While bricks snap together and apart
heirs to this future roll by in twos
breezes pinken cheeks
which cool only when sat in alcoves, to take the sun

sleeping like cats, not listening but porous

concrete apparent
a woodgrained lick
of th'uncoooked mixture

but lo!   what a pudding!
                            to pull at wrists
what a roughly nutbuttered slab
to beckon at the fat pads behind shoulders
shades of iron filings haunt the mouth
                            drag of the lode
there, where eyelids stop and the rest of the world begins
&, reversingly, at the knees' proud gristle. Diploid. Divine & this.

When nothing, there was nothing
left undone in the early
noon or after

When nothing
They would find cause
Betimes

To skim along a width of it
Innerarm bared to its teeth

When nothing
Dallying in the stairwell
Leaning too long

Later
Having been   no place
These angles, restorative:

restored.

Turnpikes 1

only go so far. There is only such a distance. Her eyes only open so wide. Her neck only torques so tight. There are only so many words. She thinks only until the edges of the lockup. She paints only Hard-Edge. Sews only jags of tesselate geometries. She works a thread too fine for any fingers. Winces at knots. Pulls at them beneath lids crêped so that everything shreds, falling and further still from the table and her nails grow friable from all the furious blind wilful heedless snagging and tearing and her prints are rubbed almost away and faint cracks are prised open by unwonted air and terrible tiny pinknesses gape and beg for extension and **she can only go so far.**

She is not without fear. There is only such a distance. She stirs to find everything in the floorplan rearranged. All change all change. The blue twangs up and away. Ozone rushes to fill the vacuum. Her shoulders are wet but she does not dare to stand to find a towel. Retint is global. The furniture stands proud, its every vertex ruffed by an infrathin scything of paper. Pressedout. Without alternatives directions she can only keep straight, cleaving to the route mapped by prior geographers, trusting to metastasizing contours though the guardrail—sticky— has slipped left and so salt is spraying right up and into her twitching nostril, and **she is not without fear.**

While she sleeps, new steel sprouts. She stirs to find the floorplan rearranged. Fittings have been remoulded to curb new insertions. The hill that was, isn't. Low alpines are already bedded in. Their roots insinuate, indiscriminate. There is even moss. Nowhere is there clear line of sight. Lenses swerve near to far. Bile rolls tidal with each creaking jump convergence. She cannot be sure that this was her orientation on retiring. She does not know it for the same bed, until she sniffs the sheets and they do not jar at least and so she pulls a flattened still clammy pillow across her face which is tautening like drying canvas and **while she sleeps, new steel sprouts.**

3 Poems

Norman Weinstein

JAZZ LIES I: CORNETIST FREDDIE KEPPARD DIES NIGHTLY FOR YOUR LISTENING PLEASURE

What was so funny Freddie Keppard?
1922
alone with a spray of baby's breath
warding off spells   lucky botanical compressed
inside gold
art deco cigarette
box/

here, hold
it, weighty as Congolese meteorite
about
to strike   smokes across lifeline in palm   streaking becomes comet
or cornet
smearing blues/

diagrams a come
lately bed

by half hour
rates with
bidet?   no
matter   Climb in

side his horn's
bell
wobbly ass first/

just try
in spite of how easy
dying by vibrating lies

just blow
& get
happy

JAZZ LIES II: THE MYSTERY OF SAN FRANCISCO MUSIC WEEK

speakeasy's corner covered by an under
exposed photograph of six year old prim
waifs, errant orphan Buster Brown, rag

tag choir on brink of shrill song, say, "School
Days" rising jeer at thrashing hickory sticks,
conductor baton tossed at off keys. There's

school corridor in stark cobalt light awaiting
their frantic back from recess march. Enter
that corridor-coffin and nails scratch black

boards as payback. But insert your face into
blurred photographic zone where their treble
trembling voices make of San Andreas a gliding

descending bass shake. Their audience drowning
in easy sentiment already welcome the next
act. Coleman Hawkins unlikely as it seems, walks

in stage left with a casual chorus of their song,
gutsy guttural gusto, always late for home
room. Arbitrary comma to their exclamation

points. But if these words spell a corridor, cobalt
light fountaining, who's supposed to straighten
photo's crookedness on bar wall? How about you, Buster?

step out of your long death & in home
coming, ask waifs at the bar if they'd welcome
a tango with likes of you, or Hawkins, or any

glowing bone bag counting 1, 2, 3, 4, ,now make
yourself pretty, then might as well be naked,
shake

JAZZ LIES III: NO NIGHT IN TUNISIA IN ARRESTED MOTION

For Antonella Anedda

Bernini folds – but accidental   since here's a thread-bare cotton
sheet under which Tunisians, some parents of what
children who can say?   hiding
under its creases from ceaseless interrogators. Am just witness

to their border crossing? Camera-Eye? Heart's shutter
shudders when they're
caught. Here, insist, take my identity wrapped up in
wronged assumptions work permits. Accept that accordion

folding this page draws
forth no tune
to survive by. But drawing
a night sky shimmering locates hymns & comforts. An unraveling

bed sheet might have been
frozen host in Bernini's
final gaze. Whether he thought
its creases lovely you & I wrap in mind

these Tunisians in his flowing
sheet. In poem's crinkling wake
bent trumpet sounds home key of
"A Night in Tunisia" – in arrested motion – arrests their betrayers

Wave

(four definitions between Canterbury and the Great Plains)
for Geraldine Monk

Nancy Gaffield

a) *A movement in the sea or other body of water by which
a portion of water rises above normal level at the same time
traveling greater or smaller distances.*

Imagine a sea of glass
an indigo sky   two waves
traveling head to head
        passing through
                        without disturbance
a civil dawn
sun wedged six degrees below the horizon's
edge
        path
                of least resistance

                old wave   old swell
                I straddle you
                feeding on your shrill krill

b) A long, convex strip of land between two broad hollows; a
    rounded ridge of sand or snow formed by the action of the
    wind.

        O ghost speak low
of the plains' undulating emptiness where
snow fences tune
the wind but the tumuli
underground are missile sites
and the clock is set
        it is three minutes
        to midnight

I walk around   learning

                                        it's peaceful
                                        with a good dog
                                        some trees

        that pivot in the hip
I know the contours of this place
        see the fragments
                Alamogordo glass

Drumpf says
        oh we're gonna build that wall
I say
        we will tear it down

I walk around extra-vagrant
        vigilant

c) A forward movement of a large body of persons (chiefly
    invaders or immigrants over-running a country, or soldiers
    advancing to an attack). This either recedes or returns after
    an interval, or is followed after a time by another body
    repeating the same movement.

Imagine a moving ridge or
swell of water
between two troughs

rollers
    in rough conditions

constructive interference
    magnifies the amplitude
        of the individual wave

cross-channel traffic
    ciphers
        cast adrift in inflatable dinghies

cross-channel traffic
    indefatigable
taking on
water

    on the tarmac a child
    draws the outline of her mother
    she takes off her shoes and
    places them
    next to her mother's
    feet   she curls herself inside
    in the shape of a question mark
        her mother soothes her to sleep

when an incident wave train hits a boundary wall
    neither hard nor soft
it slinks away snake-like
    as part of the wave is absorbed
        and part reflected

    d) *A change of atmospheric pressure or temperature consisting*
       of the gradual rise and fall and fall and rise taking place
       successively on the earth's surface.

Imagine cold arctic air
clashing
with the warm air of the south

open door feedback

> I step out
> into ghost woods
> at nautical twilight
>> the sun tipped twelve degrees
>> below the skyline

am flint
>> pierced
am hagstone
believed to bring good fortune or to ward off evil
the skin is a costume and I am no single
>> pronoun

am oriel
>>> fulsome as the moon
>> opened

am coccolith and feldspar
the erratic dream-life of debris
>> lapping
clapotis   //   skating
on thin ice

>> ribbon of blue
>>> wind blows
>>>> east to west
fracturing into spiral
acceleration

>>>>>>> we're not going to fix this up
>>>>>>> too easy

Oceanic Manta Ray

☆

Stuart Cooke

thin fossil moving years into midnight / into the Mobulidae the largest ray the shape of blood beating and cells dividing tracing continent and island / shapes a mucus sketch planktivores

zooplankton

copepods

mysid shrimps

arrow worms

bottom feeder water strainer youm build the vortex / with whalesharks suck it in we kill for the russet sponge in yourm gills / youm hide in the pelagic / bathe at seamounts and reefs

a rippling a metabolic essay flapping slowly over plains / the present grips like a bar--
slides swept and glimmer for moon swallow and / dive the dark heaves yourm emergent
wandering global / hugging coasts with regular upswellings / island groups offshore pinnacles
as if from a dream / they merge again into nowhere

youm speak the weight of the alien planet
to tell youm about my life of land we keep breathing this minute atmosphere
for prayer frilling to points slow wave / swoop slow wave swoon I want
complexity that territory from which we strayed in our quest
indomitable spark of message the crossed threshold of lexical
that whole plane slicing human from the canvas with spear's
spear of melody in an eye eyed by chest dance
wave swoon blabble blurbs chuckle dirge deep pitch song humid
undulating ready to close back into slow wave swoop slow
a node across species parasites and remoras a split a black slip
of yourm great brain slowly mating social travelling
by powerful beats bending yourm bowl of truths with the weight
a life of perpetual motion driven
youm stop youm sink slowly through the column
dom yourm knowing leaves me with shadow / if
geology of contrary response gifted with size wis-
calm youm feel the floor through water's reverb a
youm slice gritty field introduce big

nacle swims until youm breach flight with magical wing muscle / wavering spill of dripping light
sight / flexible fibres glimmering fantasies of raggedy drift / their fluid contours leathery pulse
grow bigger but cut from our tiny minds
into dark space / greeny and
                    cleaving

colour-morphed / dark
on the upper surface
black to grey-blue and brown
a T-pattern a black/white divide
no gradient pale
undersides spot patterned
unique patterns of blotches and scars
a dormant spine
at the base of the tail

tagged by a storm of slender fingers
each silver stroke of wake
gobbles yourm merest refuse
youm're floating island / oasis
parasites thrive all over yourm body
inside yourm pharynx yourm / gills
around yourm mouth slopping / in the mucus
on yourm back

the world's itchy / feeds on youm
in ectoparasites drags on youm
in hitchhikers / the remora sucks
into abrasions and sores
the constant burn of remora swarm
around and inside yourm bulk

cleaners set up shop at outcrops and bommies
youm beeline to visit
with plenty of time
to play in slow circuits

if a bite's too hard
youm fly into speed
a stream of fleeing cleaners
pouring from yourm body

and:
blue-streaked and lunar
tailed wrasse trail
behind
flood yourm surface
venture deep into yourm function

and:
two pale remora
cling upside down
with dorsal fin-cum-suction
cup

and:
three tiny trevally
golden in the gloom
bow riding the pressure of yourm head
like dolphins
piloting yourm voyage
from yourm dark shelter

and:
a clarion angelfish cleans
ectoparasites from yourm tail
off Mexico

appearing to balance on yourm tail youm stand above the

sea bed the cleaner fish scurry / three slender remoras circle around yourm unusual statue

    if I called to youm once les llamé en castellano: manta, manta / that cloak that blanket

that blanket-like trap I once used to catch youm
       if I see youm from the shore youm're close to shark but flapping lolling / shy as an

asymptote a blob of dark paint a submerged slick heading south with the sweep

'Oceanic Manta Ray' contains echoes of phrases from the following poems:
'the shadow's keep', by John Anderson
'Rays', by Rose Lucas
'Poem Written after September 11, 2001' & 'Poem Written from November 30, 2002, to March 27, 2003', by Juliana Spahr

Two Poems

Norman Fischer

The Quest the Hope the Journey the End

I begin at the beginning of my feelings or that is my perceptions in this case
the sound the sweet sound of something in my ear.
Hope is colorful
where there's nothing to hope for
Where there's a will there's a way where there's a way there's hope.
Now I'm out the door trailing after my imagination that's like soap to my ears
So much to disconnect from!
Probably I'm not leaning far enough in my seat to touch the body of the person in the next seat
who's also shopping
Writing poems in regular sentences with periods at the end of them indicating pause a complete
thought
is nice. Restful. Then another sentence
can begin. And give you the feeling that all this is proceeding in a way that's getting us some-
where as the plot thickens
Here a reader may well complain that not much is happening the poet is merely
pointing to the fact of the poem itself. This would be a valid
critique. It's as if there's no one here but the poem itself writing itself
of course I'm here you're here.
Now there's brilliant sunlight on the hillside no snow on the wings of airplanes on a runway in
El Paso. What's not here in your life or mine or in the life of the poem is as important as what is.

What meaning or message is a poem supposed to convey?

Vladivostok would be an example of a city I've never been to. My mind is small smaller than this walnut resting in the palm of my hand.

Wonderful greens like chard I like to eat them but even more to see them growing tall under the sun a long row of green chard pumping life every minute on the farm in the sun. But often it is foggy on the farm. The farm depends on rain. Food is good.

The palm is closed that's mysterious and when I open it there's nothing I've been concealing in it it's disappointing. I've got various ideas and commitments and principles that rule the way I make my poems or at least I did until a few minutes ago now I've got none. So I'll begin again

Innocently. This is

the first word

I've ever

uttered. Reader, do not

wonder or worry about this the envelope of my body is a husk upon which the cosmos collapses. Daigan's going was not typical. For so many days he didn't eat or drink.

Going coming what can anyone say? "I guess I must be dying all my friends are coming to say 'hi.'"

That's how you can tell. Every warm greeting from every friend means you are dying. So we use these simple words to tell ourselves we notice

we are here as if

we were. All this time i can't figure. Every word so plain. Ravaged I suppose by passing as cars each other in the road their relative

speeds. This is only a method.

Nothing passes really electrons fly away around and never go.

Where could they go?

Here I am. I don't

know what I am doing yet I body forth courageously hoping

for the best along with the rest. It's spring. Even in California this means

life's awakening plants pump more life in response to more

light

from above. I wish always wish for more. But there's never there

couldn't ever be more there could only be as much as there is this that's here

in front of me — one word or maybe two to ponder. I wish

for seas and look here are seas austere in their blueness as far as the eye can see it until the

blue of the sky

with maybe a scrap of cloud or two borders them

in fainter blue thus time and mind fade blue on blue.

So the country of mice or people say straining toward their ideas of goodness. A gentle breeze

wafts in from the open window today as I enter the plaza and climb the bandstand

that lives in another poem. Passing through the curtain between the two poems I come back to

this poem in which I'm bobbing in a boat at sea. As if I know where I am or where I'm going.

Somehow there seems sense to it all as if time like an ink spot made a stain on my shirt. It has

shape. Dark.
Angled branches of a tree against a brick building gazed at from below. A wrought iron
chair on a hill outside my window. A tree green and unmoving tells me
how to be dignified enough to simply care for myself and all
the other sad news around here.
Diction
makes it happen
but this poem was never about
my feelings never about
my meanings. Look — a guy
with a leaf-blower just
walked by and I—
I too in my grief and wonder
search tirelessly for perfection and find it.

The Urgency

That would be a failure of nerve
Umm..... can't see above the dunes contrary
If there's no ruling or prevailing idea
It's just a case of graphomania
I'll cut up a few more for dinner
At long last just anything at all satisfies
So how choose — relax
About it there can be a crack or even
More than one. Don't
Pester her any more than you have to
The two of us talking over the transom

5 from *Graphic Novella: Collage and Gloss*

Rachel Blau DuPlessis

How to write? But the very letters are coming loose! A ball of gibberish falls out. Is that thing on the bottom a clue or a clew? This a detective story? It says it is. We might be doubly deceived. Is it plausible that the teller of the story, the detective in this plot "did it"? Like *The Murder of Roger Ackroyd.* Can we stand another tour de force?

Say instead that this is graphic. This is a novella. The eternal is a hopeless rag. The symmetrical an already rejected goal.

Call this "news"--news of a novelty that is not a novel. News of a poetry that is not a poem. It's true that the novelties and novelty of a different novel (another poem) are no longer really novel, although they always may amuse. It's smaller than a novel, and graphic. Even too explicit. But the pictures sometimes go wrong way round. It's all uglier and more inept than art. Trash book. "What is the new" has long been the question, and "how to make it." But really, who now is satisfied by a category called "the new"? As such, it is a fake, if perpetually charming as it offers the happy pleasure of being on top of things. This color, that cut, maybe some sequins. That face, this leg. Gratifying. But overly stylized, like flipping through a magazine. The issue is "the news." Even just the small news, the bits we titrate for a small dose of reading so we don't dissolve in the acid bath of disaster. The smaller news is feeling the sadness of an endless beginning continuing, and in suspension. No real sequence. It's true that there is a specific flag draped in this snapshot--but it's meant to head up just one file among many. True--this one's the file I am slotted in. What are you writing in those awkward letters? Is something happening? Certainly a perpetual rage at uncontainable inhuman humanity. Shorelines? "The ███████ regime's bloody crackdown on pro-democracy demonstrators has prompted a volta-face in ████████." Violent unstable weather? Extractionism that cracks the earth asunder? The endless deaths of bees? Sand for water? Many people are observing. Can see these events. Live in watchfulness. Somaticize dissonant vibrations. Sey.

But few as yet have particularly new ("novel") ways of behaving. Certainly not most of those in power. The collapse of the political class--and not simply in one place--is now patent. Public good twists to private gain. They are selling the state to high rollers. And molding citizens into clumps of wastage and confusion. The roaring and rearing of economic elites will hardly compensate. This collapse of institutions--but we're in the twenty-first century, how can this be?--it seems a shocking science fiction! Who expected these murky and weasely sets of post-disaster denials: "I'm not responsible." "Nor I!" "It just is." "We cannot stop it." "What can we do?" "Very important people support this _____ (factory, mine, dam, investment, atomic energy installation, etc.)." There are experts on the case. Their experts are on the case. All this extraction and extra action provides jobs, infrastructure (sometimes) (rarely) (not for general use) (restricted) (this was "unforeseen" when we agreed to it). Laws have been rewritten and barely noticed. Just more wordy words, we thought. You seem to benefit, OK. Then "the laws" get interpreted; we are stunned at the result. Oceans are implicated. The vastness of this roiling event is impossible and implausible. And yet we are here. It thus seems true that "We are on our own"--but that's also absolutely impossible, and implausible. What is to be done? Will we drown in the sudden rising of intemperate waters? It seems that every initiative is half finished, half collapsed. Partial--and again, cui bono? Who benefits? If this is the question, and the answers are partially findable, why are there no sanctions? Why are shifts and changes so meager? How can one even begin to write this--is it only to imitate the half-collapsed? The helpless hand? 0 0 0 that corny poetics of mimesis. And the glue itself will wrinkle and pucker. Nothing will be artful. Nothing pleasant. Nothing temperate. It is not a particularly aesthetic moment. TO SAY THE LEAST. Sey.

The materials on the recto side were all clipped from one random issue of *The Philadelphia Inquirer,*Thursday, June 13, 2013, from pages Al-A6 only.

I just sit somewhere, wherever
I am found,
seriously
making poor art --I'm
serious; artpoor, arte povera,
art spoor, the art from small
materials, from detritus of convention,
from the underseen, underwanted, the
less and less.
A scrap, a bit, a shred, a shard, a headline
ripped to isolate one word, a word
(a sword, a surd, a sort) that gives me the fantods.
I cut things shabbily, trusting chance,
but also, and always, suspiciously.
I used too wet a glue, innocently.
I'd "watered it with my tears."
I cited things, like from Grenier,
then crumpled them, then
flattened them out.
Sey. Just scratches
of days, nothing much.
Not looking for a lot of "results."
This is a vague (unplotted)
archive, neither omnivorous
nor complete.
Yes.
Sey.

#
She discovered her own complexity with some regret.
Mazel tough.

#
She taunts the story
ambitiously non-hegemonic.

An eros of conviction laid out some detritus.

#
Setting. Mustn't forget setting. Raining. Dark. Forested (forested? I'm at the desk!). Dry
and hard. Wet and lush. Symbolic . A book on the table. A chocolate bar. Not spring yet.
Setting one thing here, another there. Window with a dirty screen. Lists of things to do.
Night. Day. Time frame. A ladder. Apt. App store open. Beholden. Someone walking
down on the street. Is that person part of the story? Or random? I can't believe you are
so ignorant of the right way to go about this.

Fraying a path, while burrowing to the end of weariness.

There is no "whole" as such. One curlicue, one excessive note, mark, intonation, spelling error, interpretive or suggestive cadence, one bit of fancy or willfulness, one key association of words and the "whole" exceeds itself, displacing its ideal message. But this displacement is the actual state of things.

(And thus all books are of another mind.)

Dance the jaunty dance of understanding. These legs are dapper and admirable. Wellclothed, actually. Their power is charming and meant to charm.

The harm here is harder to track. It pleads and elaborates; the tone is unbearable. It's confused about cause and effect, ends and means, agent and client, A and not-A, and who does what to whom.

The stakes rise later, both for (the cool) authorities and for those who are jerked around. For the knowledgeable and the baffled--for both. Even if they hardly know it

(given the fashion shot glossiness vs. the flyer photocopied and stuffed in the streetcorner news boxes of the free papers as a kind of psychic journalism, knowledge consolidation, or reportage),

they are on the same page.

\#
Wake up Philadelphians:

Read people, know sad, glad, upset, sick worried breathing. Would not want elderly
woman a prisoner in camper trailer Van. Stealing love is crime as stealing book. Tell
truth and things go right. Each person pays for own errors. Doctors are to help patients
Teachers are to help students. A scout to help lonly kid on own street. A Mother is first
to help own daughter. A Dad to help son. So stay alert. It is urgent to find out what's
going on in own family. Psychiatrists are to make many suggestions. Do you. . . .
Develop positive thinking: Think Good. Do Good. SOMETHING SEEMS WRONG HAVE
COURAGE TO SPEAK UP. THANK YOU FOR READING THIS.

"Pages from different moments are bound together"
pages from different monuments
sometimes they add up.

I decided to swim 50 fixed lengths, an unbelievable self-improvement scheme, and had started doing just this, but in a light yellow pique bathing suit with a full 360-degree circle skirt over what we used to call the pippick--yes, reader, it was a fashionable garment from the actual 1950s. Pond mud swelled the hem, dirtying the folded pique edging. The skirt created mucho drag. This was being a girl back then.

I wish I could make a gigantic pique mock-up of that bathing suit, 100 times original size, both as a conceptual work and a work of enormous craft, to be hung outside the entrance facade of every major museum in the ...

oh, forget it.

\#

The women students at the museum school were tired of being groped, felt up, brushed against, butts touched, talked at with aggressive pleasantries during the crits, or during his studio class. Given that things like this were suddenly being discussed more openly, they came together and decided to "do an action" to confront this artist, their teacher. So they bought a can of white latex paint, and one day they stood in a gauntlet, painty hands dripping, and as he walked down the corridor, they groped him. *Pudeur* kept

them from grabbing at his crotch, so the result was that his jacket--his jeans jacket--was enormously covered with handprints, messy blotches and streaks of white paint. And he was upset beyond their wildest imaginings: "This jacket belongs to Dennis Oppenheim!!" "This is Dennis Oppenheim's jeans jacket! He loaned it to me!" He was so upset that many of the women felt quite badly about the jacket. So some took the jacket and washed it for him. But two women objected vehemently and refused to help the other women wash it.

from *Late Arcade*

Nathaniel Mackey

——————————————   17.IV.84

Dear Angel of Dust,

It seemed if I could only 1) angle at the exact amount of incline, 2)
lard lead-in with absence in the most parsed and plotted manner
possible, lace or load it in such fashion as to make tread trepidatious,
the ground trepidatious, trepidation the ground itself, 3) titrate touch
in such a way as to build while disbursing twinge, verge on twinkle
perhaps, 4) coax or connive, eke sound out, so situate twitch or its
adumbration as to extenuate love's least integer, so reside within
extenuation as to mitigate timbral collapse, 5) wring the notes as
much as play them, *wring* fully in league with an implied play on *toll*,
twist each note as though it were cloth and the drop squeezed out of
it both, 6) placate momentum's demand while recruiting an abiding
pocket, a cyst or an insistence indigenous to suasion or swell, 7)
confess to a certain dismay or admit my impatience, pound against
time until the beat wore ragged, 8) ply layers of waywardness, an
annunciative ken peppered with and paced by hesitancy throughout,
an arrhythmic hitch cognate or conjugal with nothing if not rhythm,

9) be at large in a twilit fallback, relaxed albeit beset by combinatory chagrin, fallen shade's fluency and fount, all would be right with the world.

    All would be right, at the very least, I thought, with the solo I was at the beginning of. By combinatory chagrin I meant a sense I've gotten in dreams, the sense of returning to a place I've been to before, dreamt of before, dreamt I've been to outside of dreams before, as though to dream was not to make up scenery but to traverse and revisit stable terrain, actual ground and what's built on it, this or that house, this or that room inside. These houses give off the feel of a combination of houses, places I've lived or visited given an odd yet familiar aspect, teasingly familiar but not to be precisely placed. Something about the approach to one of these houses might suggest the promontory to a friend's house in Pasadena while, once inside, the stairway to the second floor would recall, ever so faintly, that of the flat I lived in in Oakland, and so on. One of these rooms might seem compounded of the living room of our apartment in Miami when I was a child, the library cubby I studied in when I was in college and more. It's as if all the aspects, facets and features of these places were bits of glass in a kaleidoscope, subject to changing arrangement and permutation while maintaining a sense of real premises, real provenance, more than simply concocted, more than merely dreamt-up.

    Chagrin, though, in that, coming upon or coming into these places, I always feel I've forgotten something I meant to remember. These rooms, halls and houses appear to be part of some mnemonic practice, a memory theater of the sort Frances Yates writes about perhaps. I despair each time that I've lost the key that would unlock the familiarity I sense but can't entirely call forth, the legend that would mete out place and punctuality, dispel the tease or taunt of what appears partly "on," partly "off." In some of these dreams I feel like a ghost in the Winchester House, combinatory largesse only so many stairways and doors that lead nowhere. I feel toyed with, the Bible's "In my Father's house are many mansions" brought to mind, a trickster's pitch.

    So it was with the notes and sonic tactics at my disposal at my solo's outset. Even so, I wanted to step onto such oneiric ground and into such oneiric housing, have my solo be the means of doing so or even be such ground and housing, my own such instructed tenancy and tread. I wanted to be like the man spoken of in my antithetical opera, "both hands tied, trying to build a house with his voice while sitting on a cot in his jail cell." I wanted my solo, by the time I was done, to say what Rick Holmes used to say on KBCA, "We have built!" I was bent on a masonic outcome for my chagrin.

This was during a gig at The Studio we finished a few hours ago. We were playing "Like a Blessed Baby Lamb." I was on soprano. We'd recently played it at the Come Back Inn and we go back to it now and then at rehearsals. We've played around with different instrumentations, different ways of voicing it, and Lambert wanted to give one of the new ones a try at the gig—him on tenor, me on soprano, Penguin on alto clarinet, Aunt Nancy on violin, Djamilaa on harmonium and Drennette on tablas. How to open up and open out from the gruff stamp Archie put on the piece and how to work the time in a way that keeps to a certain signature drag (as though tar were stuck to the soles of our shoes) but keeps to it otherwise is what we've been asking. How to get gruff stamp and signature drag to coexist with Eastern sinuosity and cut is what we've been asking.

I was the last to solo. The order was Lambert, Aunt Nancy, Penguin, Djamilaa, then me. The violin and the harmonium did exactly what we had in mind. Aunt Nancy and Djamilaa lent signature drag a vectored swell, a diagonal swell, an upward and onward tending, tumescent lilt. ("Lilt" puts it too lightly. It was nothing short of hallowed what they brought to an essentially profane wager, titular lamb notwithstanding. "Lift" says it better, "coronal lift.") They gave it a keening, devotional air, Drennette's tablas adding duly acute prance, due traction. This they did without speeding up the tempo, turning signature drag into Baul-Bengali saunter.

Djamilaa's solo had drawn us into a sacred cave, drawn us in and drawn us in effigy on its walls. It was a crystal cave, a sphere rayed out in all directions like fireworks exploding, shooting radii the spokes of a ball that would swell and contract, the harmonium's bellows lungs and hallows both. Things had gotten religious, as in fact, Djamilaa implied or insisted, they always are. She had taken the title's wager to heart. When she finished and the applause died down, the ground I found myself on, the cave I found myself in, gave me pause. I stepped into my solo with a phobic, philosophic tread, a duly fearful tread.

I tend toward Pharoah's way of playing soprano. I like a little constriction in my sound, long on shading, not the tabula rasa sound we were taught was the goal. I like a nasal burr or a nasal buzz along the edges, a bit of abrasion. The soprano's ability to glide, the auto-pilot sense it can fall into, needs to be guarded against, as does its ability to soar. Room has to be made for creak and squeal, subdued crackle, a ducklike sotto voce, not without an R&B twinge. Pharoah tends to glide and soar more than I felt was called for, so it was Wayne's ictic, foraging way on "Dindi," which, as you know, I've never gotten over and will never get over, that was more the tack I took. It was a more grounded sound I sought or at least a sound that sought to be grounded, a sound that felt its way, even groped its way, seeking ground.

Djamilaa's harmonium had subsided to a carpetlike lowing, ecumenical seep and support. Aunt Nancy's violin was a holding action, airborne glimmer if not watery glare atop distant asphalt on a summer day. Drennette's tablas partly kept time, partly bought it, marking it no matter which, a pinged, ringing press or appeal that tolled an announcement of dues accrued. I stepped cautiously into this coven or cave as though barefoot on a bed of hot coals, tread nothing if not trepidation and vice versa, hesitant from heel to toe, tentative, testing. I temporized for a few bars before what I've come to call the Nine Golden Precepts, the desiderata I listed above, came to me in a flash. I repeat them here for emphasis:

THE NINE GOLDEN PRECEPTS

1. Angle at the exact amount of incline.

2. Lard lead-in with absence in the most parsed and plotted manner possible, lace or load it in such fashion as to make tread trepidatious, the ground trepidatious, trepidation the ground itself.

3. Titrate touch in such a way as to build while disbursing twinge, verge on twinkle perhaps.

4. Coax or connive, eke sound out, so situate twitch or its adumbration as to extenuate love's least integer, so reside within extenuation as to mitigate timbral collapse.

5. Wring the notes as much as play them, wring fully in league with an implied play on toll, *twist each note as though it were cloth and the drop squeezed out of it both.*

6. Placate momentum's demand while recruiting an abiding pocket, a cyst or an insistence indigenous to suasion or swell.

7. Confess to a certain dismay or admit my impatience, pound against time until the beat wears ragged.

8. Ply layers of waywardness, an annunciative ken peppered with and paced by hesitancy throughout, an arrhythmic hitch cognate or conjugal with nothing if not rhythm.

9. Be at large in a twilit fallback, relaxed albeit beset by combinatory chagrin, fallen shade's fluency and fount.

After temporizing for those few bars, I went on, I can say without bragging, to make good on all nine.

I'm not saying this was the best or the most dazzling solo I've ever taken. There's something about the Precepts coming to me the way they did, incumbent upon me all of a sudden as if I took dictation, a suddenly scribal providence or at least provision on the tips of my fingers, on my lips, teeth and tongue, on my diaphragm and in my lungs, that made it get to me and stay with me, still stay with me, to such an extent I haven't been able to get to sleep. Was it the suddenly scribal providence or provision or was it Djamilaa sitting on the floor crosslegged and lotuslike before the harmonium, dress modestly pulled over her knees, covering her open thighs, that did and does it? Was it the unquenchable glimpse I closed my eyes and imagined I got of what lay under her dress, the bulge of hair beneath cotton or silk, such fit I felt exhorted by, rich beard and lift and betweenness, that did and does it? Was it that the harmonium seemed as much incense holder as axe, the ecumenical seep and support it disbursed as much musk as music, the very floataway musk Djamilaa's nightie dilated Dredj's nostrils with? Was it that I could've sworn I sniffed it wafting from under her dress, a newly mixed Vedic neroli, an infusive attar, an infinitely penetrant perfume? Was it this that did and does it?

It was all these things. Djamilaa is my muse and will always be, the someone I need and will need on my bond, as the old song says. She led and leads me thru love's long-tenured bazaar, love's late arcade. Whatever probity, whatever duly theophobic tread, theophanic tread, I acquitted myself with (and my solo did, I know, do nothing if not that), I owe to her inspiration. The Nine Golden Precepts themselves, I'm sure, were the work of her inspiration. Even now, going on five in the morning, I feel I can't but be longer with it.

The Golden Precepts readied my way. Such bearings as they gave me gotten, I left off temporizing with an annunciative, almost airless flutter, a fledgeling, asthmatic burst whose asthmaticity rhetorically asked how to speak of things of which one does not speak. Aunt Nancy, Drennette and Djamilaa knew this to be rhetorical, understood it as a preamble to doing exactly that. We would indeed speak the unspeakable Drennette affirmed with a run of karate chops to the tablas, shunting my almost airless flutter along. Aunt Nancy and Djamilaa were likewise all horizontality, Aunt Nancy with a series of tonic-tending bowswipes, Djamilaa with a sirening ride of the harmonium's high end.

That played or that said, I told myself, "Take your time." I let my embouchure go loose as I played the first seven notes of the head, cutting it off as if interrupted by a better option than mere completion, had at or put upon by some lateral enchantment. Aunt Nancy's bow was that enchantment, as commanding as Cupid's arrow, picking up and repeating the first five of those notes, identification, if not identity, up to more than identification. Djamilaa meanwhile settled into a low-lying, mist-on-the-moors creep, a droning amble ever close to the floor, the stage floor it made feel earthen, rolling earth. Drennette had increasing recourse to the heels of her hands on the tablas, coaxing a fat sound out of them, all reach and rotundity, itself a rolling aspect as well, fat wheels we rode.

My loose embouchure caught air and the vibrating reed was a drill or a jackhammer against my teeth, bodily abidance's dues, I meant to insist or insinuate, nothing more. Djamilaa, who knew my mouth as no one knew my mouth and whose recondite musk had my nose open, at once caught my insinuation. She answered with a skein of sound, a ribbon of sound, still close to the earthen floor, bodily abidance's reap or condolence. She pulled it from the harmonium's bass register, a grumbling, organlike run Alice Coltrane would've been proud to call her own.

The Nine Precepts ushered me along, Djamilaa's undulance

under cloth an abiding bond and trust, rolling bulge, rolling fit, rolling traipse I felt furthered by, a whiff-quickened wraith of myself chasing myself. Robert Johnson's hell hounds were a walk in the park up against the chase I gave myself, a counterintuitive, slow-tempo chase I now tightened my embouchure to ante up on—eked-out advance, eked-out inveterate lag, eked-out inconsequence.

I took my time. My sound opened up, unpinched, not the zero degree at which the horn extends the esophagus without seam or serration, the sound Oliver Nelson, for example, gets on soprano, but less given to the pulverous fray around its edges I started with. Dust off a moth's wing was there to be heard even so, but less of it, my sound as open-throated as it gets. It was cool, collected, not entirely without strain but backing away from it, pointedly announcing a parting of ways with it. I thought of when I was a kid and of my mother's friend Mary who'd always say, when things were getting to her, "I can't be strainin'-up here," which was always exactly what she was doing. Everyone called her Strainin'-up Mary. Strainin'-up soprano was the horn I blew.

Things were getting to me. The coven or the cave I'd been inducted into or stepped into played briar patch to my Brer Rabbit, no place I more wanted to be. Announcedly not strainin'-up, I remained calm and collected, my backing away from strain belied by moth-wing dust though it was. Even as things got to me in what was at bottom a good way, my response above bottom was nothing if not mixed. Cool and collected as I was, I played scared, wanted to be scared and grew scared of the very place I wanted to be, feet shod, so to speak, in theophobic, theogonic tread. Djamilaa, Drennette and Aunt Nancy, my three witches, were divinatory and divine in laying down, ladies though they were, the brer patch it was now incumbent on me to traverse.

I couldn't be strainin'-up but I was ever so detectably strainin'-up, moth-wing dust my boon and my betrayal. Strainin'-up Mary was to me as Trane's Cousin Mary had been to him or as Horace Tapscott's Drunken Mary had been to him, a makeshift Madonna or a makeshift Magdalene or a third, entirely makeshift muse for the occasion. Cauldron Mary I wanted to rename her, a fourth, faraway witch in league with the three with whom I played, but Drennette, sensing this it seemed, gave one of the tablas, which might as well have been my head, a resounding slap. I stood by tradition and stayed with "Strainin'-up."

Horace's Mary was more than a passing thought. Strainin'-up Mary was known to have a drink or two or three throughout the day. "Drunken Mary's" head seemed exactly the groove to "Like a Blessed Baby Lamb's" tongue, so I paired it now with the full first ten notes of the latter's head, a joint or a joining I parsed out using Horace's tipsy waltz-time approach. This gave it as much jaunt as our slow tempo could accommodate. We did so without at all speeding up.

I bleated lamblike, reminiscent of Wayne's "Dindi," a connect-the-dots tack with which I stated the two heads, conjugated the two heads, all the while observing the Nine Precepts to the letter. Djamilaa's bellowing hallows put me in churchical stead, though Aunt Nancy's wicked bowswipes and bowsweeps were yet another matter, as were Drennette's crescendoing tabla slaps, not to mention a certain way in which I scared myself. My tipsy traverse of the brer patch was, by turns and at times concurrently, god-fearing, goddess-fearing, witch-fearing, propriophobic, whichever as the case might be.

Strainin'-up Mary showed me the way. She magnified and illumined the way the Nine Precepts had made ready. I staggered, bounding laterally and at times diagonally between lamblike bleat and capric slur, Djamilaa's goatlike beauty a heady brew aligned with Strainin'-up's unsecured walk. I stole a peek at her seated at the harmonium. She shot me a grin. Undulance under cloth, I couldn't help noticing, had nowhere near subsided. "Waft be thy name," I hummed into the horn, a recourse to heteroglossic traipse Djamilaa met with harmolodic tryst, sounding organlike again, Larry Young meets Ornette.

Drennette was all fingertips now, digital dispatch and acrobatic display, a boon to my every capric slur. I walked sonically cool and collected even so, incongruous capric aplomb. Had I been walking nonsonically I'd have turned sideways and dragged a leg, harked back to a dance we did when I was a kid called The Stroll, a dance that danced us as much as we danced it, a dance I've never been able to shake. Thus the slur, the slide away from collectedness, its merger with incongruous aplomb.

Aunt Nancy picked up on Drennette's fingertip attack and went from arco to pizzicato, from swipe and sweep to pinch and pluck. Djamilaa picked up as well, now dispensing staccato runs as if at the wheel of a car, pumping the brakes. The ground we crossed was all the more a brer patch now, bristling with divinatory aspect and pop, divine, prestidigitator snap.

Brer patch was hopping ground, a dense arena rocked by ricochet, detonation, ignition. Vex and revisitation ran side to side, to and fro. I lowered the horn and pointed its bell at the floor, bent over the way I've seen Miles bend over, listening for a certain sound. I was still all lamblike bleat and capric slur, at the brer patch's mercy it seemed I was told later, coaxed, baited and beset by prestidigitator bristle, pinch and pop. I wanted a hollowed-out sound if not a hallowed or haloed sound, moth-wing dust mixed and congealed with ambient humidity, for all its airborne humors a conical or cylindrical wrap of paste.

A conical or cylindrical compress applied to the open wound the air itself now was, the sound I wanted was buoyed by Aunt Nancy, Djamilaa and Drennette's brer patch rotunda, churchical girth I tried in vain, straining, to get my arms around. Churchical girth would not be gotten around, not be embraced but at a distance, an ever so discreet hydraulics of approach it demanded, mandated. The sound I wanted was the sound I went down and got, bent over, horn pointed at the floor, an expectorant howl, no longer cool, collected, an expectorant croon that brought up a shake-the-rafters descent into the horn's low register, a rafters-rattling landing on the horn's lowest note.

The sound I wanted, not quite knowing I wanted it, was the sound of the shaken rafters, the rafters rattling. I now saw what I wanted, that this was the sound I wanted, the highest rafters of a wooden palace rattled by the note I hit and held, wood rubbed to a sheen by oneiric return and revisitation, another strangely familiar house I dreamed I was in. I didn't open my eyes and I didn't need to. I knew we were in that house, that palace. I kept holding the note (holding on, as Bobby Womack would say), doing so with circular breathing. Aunt Nancy, Djamilaa and Drennette kept their plucked and popping rotunda alive and played louder now. I knew we were in that house, that place, that palace.

The audience had begun loudly applauding as I held the note and the rotunda popped and bristled, Pharoah's "Let Us Go into the House of the Lord" having nothing on our stringent, less unctuous approach. I didn't open my eyes and I didn't let go of the note as Lambert and Penguin came back in, restating the head over my sustained note and the brer patch rotunda, only for us all to stop on a dime at head's end. We had built.

As ever,

N.

[Late Arcade *is volume five of* From A Broken Bottle Traces of Perfume Still Emanate, *an ongoing series of letters written by composer/multi-instrumentalist N., founding member of a band known as the Molimo m'Atet. Volumes one thru four are* Bedouin Hornbook, Djbot Baghostus's Run, Atet A.D. *and* Bass Cathedral.]

from *Work*

Richard Makin

XXXIII

1   We are unorchestrate. Dark columns in plastic figure, intersecting spindles of light.

Misdread: the art of setting stage or arranging an alternative pictorial motive.

Birdlife clinging to an old man in the square. Saints fly down. I'll make up my own mind about the crew.

I've got the bag with the meat in – an image captured by mercury and silver iodine. The fact that there is red ink in the well, and the packet contains a rose-coloured seed, is encouraging. A selection of short musics retell the tale. All my letters have given up.

2   The entire family has been memorialized, a tribe crammed full with coincidence. He didn't see the other side coming until it was too late. Enlarged artificially, of all the rumours in the building, this is the one.

It was so funny and so simple. What makes the adventure impressive is the way it's constructed: a great wave over the tip of the ear, between thumb and big toe; this is a production being manufactured as we speak. She moulds her characters out of silhouettes, space archaeology: the film cracks, the land splits open to reveal a chalky outcrop et cetera. . . . She cuts them out of herself; this is her sanctuary, her berth. The instructions read bring a picnic.

I woke up three hours later. She's playing a tam-tam made of crow-skin and wood, pricking at her hair, pulling off her shawl – any attempt to sustain motion – any substitute for doing nothing. She says your feathers must be caressed back to the right direction.

Everyone knows something about us – either the truth, so far as it's accessible, or some exaggerated whisper. I felt so ill I took to my bed and never looked back.

3   What about authorship, beautifully composed for the human voice? We now have a full cast of bodies. Books cling to me. I am subjected to an electric current passing between the two cells on either side of my own.

Nobody will actually speak. As I get older, the logic of suicide makes more and more sense. The sole of her foot pressed against mine.

Folk have become shy of placing.

4   It is not I. They bark, surrounding. I wrap myself in a damp blanket. The sky tilts at an impossible angle. One wall is glass brick, through which shines a dazzling white light. There's a new kind of etiquette on track, the comedy of happenstance.

5   She writes to say that she sits overlooking. Between her and the sea is an ancient pine forest and the sun strikes the surface of the water. He is looking at the same surface. That's where the sorting lies, exposed to a copper plate.

6   There's always a slight alarm when I do this. Let's move along a bit, set to the music of an occasional guess. In the parlour he sees a spinning wheel, a machine sewing up a torn face. (Please recall that you don't get paid for my privilege.) I stop and wait; in me is this metronome. You can choose from any one of these situations: build twice a house as this and so forth.

7   Our chief component is a benzine ring with attacked carbon. I work around her. The atoms are the same proposition as water. (I love the way those rasping clarinets shift in and out of focus.) I knew there was something. I find a big stone and a new kind of metal we've never heard before – its outline shines with a silver gleam. She says everything is formulaic.

In one scene a giant table descends from the sky, laden. After the deluge, random information will emerge at first; it's vital to remember, there's a stricture around her heart.

8   Keep it simple. People are snared in a relentless cycle of distraction and self-regard, an undeserved attention to the minutiae of their banal and unproductive lives. It was quite a serious situation. It was their fence. It was a good job no one got killed.

No, no, no.

9   Ah, but extend this idea to kindred. . . . I have established an arc between the two electrodes, anything for the sake of fidelity. The liver has become quite warm. And that's about it – his life is an inexact discipline.

10   Discourse invariably arrives at the neutral (before he went blind, at the age of eight). My politics are never.

11   As it happens, he isn't fit to make utterance today, having been overeaten. Any identical objects are made samer still. The brain is removed and the inside of the skull carefully cleaned of flesh.

It didn't bother me; it was behind the cooker, the oesophagus. It regenerates itself. The idea is to cultivate memory (this doesn't work). You must get bored doing something all the time.

Genes are irresponsible. An international trade barrier has been constructed.

I have explained this to you, so you should be able to understand. I was solitary back then; I did not hear the hiss of the pendulum. I will now wake the homestead, the redoubt – sweeping impartial being.

12   He's a nine-percenter, too much salt at the interstices. Nothing's my fault. So we cannot be sure without further investigation

that the gift of prophecy would also follow this pattern. Comparisons are odorous:

> *[. . .] that they shall come [. . .] Who will [. . .] he will [. . .]*

It sloshes about in its cradle of bone, precariously supported at the rim by a corona of metal antennae. Elected sniper for one day, I fetch an airgun. The origin is doubtless film. The economy collapses.

'Bring *dan-de-li-ons.*'

13   I began with my own unfathomable attraction to certain words. You can reveal everything that's to pass by studying the subject's physiognomy. His remaining kidney is piqued. The others were persuaded to leave their organs behind – cellular mucus membrane, refreshingly messianic et cetera. The sought after herb has blanched flowers, 'a matted cottony pubescence'. . . . Others have cleft palates and a solitary row of teeth.

Back with you, head-keeper, up against the wall: 'You are not the same person,' and so on. . . . They are planning to get rid of me at about the same time.

This has appeared under a number of rubrics, but I'm still relating events as they happen. I'm changing nothing; it's still razors. There's an old-fashioned light at the end. We were wading against the tide.

Just get this funeral over with, please. Put your head back on your shoulders.

14   There were two solutions. (Her grandfather.) I chose the bed because there were no people anywhere near it.

We are situated in the panic room of a sealed argument. Scale is based on the night sky.

15   Landscape with twisted river mouth. (Where's your glittering now.) The number is seven – the tail end has broken off, what's called a coda. He hustles the boy out and bangs the door to. They used a garrotte made of barbed wire at the cabin in the forecast. . . He is about to burst. I have learnt where all the rejected mail ends up.

I spell out entire sentences on the roof of my mouth with my tongue, where no one can read them. The head already has my name, my race. He's probably touching, snout to earth as we speak. I warned you we were close.

We are going to sit for a while and wait. He's tied up and then there's nothing. Only his column remains, abruptly awful. It's like that with me, the stony path at the turn.

16   *Mirrored to twist her yearning face toward camera.*
        No fellow spirit leans upon her today. The chairs are from somewhere else. I'm summoned, from a base meaning augur; pass me the drip-tray. Not one of the ants fell off the stick.
        These days his face is much the time buried in her cunt. After several hours of this, we may never hear from him again. Day here means state.

17   Shadows less sharp. Go to the top, move that little bit closer. Boy holds a pebble, a feather, and a fossiled thing from the years – pupils dilated, scattered teeth on the beach, male and female. He doesn't even turn around to look.

18   That's it, think of yourselves.

19   I am unsureness personified; I got bored withholding. When I ask for his sigil, I get the evil eye, parallel rows of cuneiform impressions, all very intimidating: puddles of mercury, the light behind the crane, isolated clouds.

20   Now here comes the big vegetable me, balanced between two plagues. I'm not here next week, or the week after (poverty of mimesis et cetera). We are in love, yet still this struggle: pathos and defiance, who have followed me about all my life.
        He reduces memory to a squatter form. The chosen shape is a pyramid atop a column with convenient slit, waves crashing beyond the harbour. Then there was a spell of monotheism, but only for a couple of days; I'm too expensive.
        There was nothing to watch over after all. The dominion originally expressed is not. He would never dream of using me to his own advantage, his own language.

21   One moves to the rear of the vehicle to empty his flask. (This is merely a series of observations of how things are.) See, you have a collision of S's.

'Oh look children, quick he's down on his hands and knee, admittedly. . . .'

This gives you a bit more flexibility and a hint of what's to come. This is what I've noticed, just by peering out: odour of fish-glue and floor polish, gimlets of strained light, impoverished flesh – he would never forget watching her body turn black through a lack of oxygen.

22   It was like a human treadmill. (Not really: centipede, hybrid dog-leg.) He outpersonates. When we were growing up, he was the only one who could become truly angry. You speak an estimate of my life.

Don't you dare touch anything that resembles this – a tense expressing the simple past, with no guarantee of continuance. We tried to reinvent this place once before: you took a lift from the top floor, straight to the molten core of the earth.

23   The other points and laughs for ten minutes straight. For him, this is a matter of philosophy – at home, shapeshifting every form, all day bent buggered over his crucibles.

The cache included Browning automatic rifles, gas canisters, bomb-sights, 90mm anti-aircraft gun directors, and 345,000 units of the 30-calibre M1 carbine rifle. On this occasion he's allowed to keep all his finds, the fossil and the other relics. Critical economic policy files have been reduced to punch cards.

This is endless. What if we agree to call this particular segment *Mythopoeia*?

24   I think he always longed. My father was found. I invigilate and never slept. Logos was stamped on most of the products.

25   Grains of glass. Splinters of mirror, a silvering – what's called the tain. I don't know what happened next. Make her sound like a revenant – shed scales under foot, the crunch of volcanic ash beside the vestry door. . . . She recoiled a step or two as the stranger advanced and clutched my arm in silence. I'm rocking my head backwards and forwards; clearly structure is collapsing. I think she's vulnerable to one or two of our components, to the inconsistency of paper, refracted light.

It was the longest disturbance; I once fell straight through to the base. There's a new domestic blow-torch on the market.

26   He rejects this uncompromising scene (my original 'unpromising' now seems preferable). They concluded that from the direct union of soil with his body a human personality could not fail to result. . . . So much for anatomy – nerves of septum, hard palate et cetera – much ringing in the ears, screams in discord.

'I am signal earth,' he says, 'there was one survivor, two dead and a 'droid smashed beyond recognition.'

I'm appointed assassin. Film is again.

'Why are you scrambling me? Any white flower will do.'

'This is no armistice [*trembling with anger*] – it's a capitulation.'

Morse it was, tapped out by bell. Ibis, cobra and jackal are tattooed across his shoulders, just the silhouettes. Do you not remember.

27   Study for plate wash, heightened with white wine and gouache, depicting a young man pulling on a rope. Another man up a ladder and a lady at the top of a house, arms out the window, as if to say, 'Where have you be?' . . . She sings a song about how tired she is of wanting.

28   Another insists on concealing. He cuts down a branch heavy with pollen. This goads my first objection. And at this instant he says 'I' for the first time.

I felt as if in trance, a rather workaday supreme being. It would compromise my task to be near you even for a moment.

29   'Do you know exactly where we are, Landgrave?'

I don't know what it means, to be supervised. Strictly speaking, you can't be anatomy if you're dead. Concrete things steadily increased, at the cost of Volunteer XII.

I'll never forget the day they came back – for a long while we sat and watched their savage chewing at raw flesh. But the background hum is always there, just above my skull. I think we need to gather together, as in the old, fingering the keys; this is a group that aren't technically mad, you understand.

The drill was found miles away. There's a memorial that floods, too close to the surface of the river, a corridor with pinpricks of light. I steal the image; I stole everything.

30   She is understate, past care. She is lost current. Leave the pebbles here, leave them be.

31   Such velocity. He guesses a path through the forest. I exist slowly and nothing interests me.

He seems to have died twice, and has now been shunted to the outer beacon – the reverse, with surfeit of eye.

'I is cursed. Who is your postilion?'

Clusters of sharp spikes are set at intervals along the spine.

32   Slow torches flicker in the dark. I am sometimes associated with customer; I remember that evening well. I'm convinced she is still in the backyard. I write. I think this arrangement can work. When it's blue outside, it is very blue.

33   I'm sorry about earlier, the murmurs. Everyone seems to have found out except me. Metal oxidizes in the air (viz your cycle spent in the rain). I am just testing. In this version – a previous seance – we have evidence of memory. I seem to pass my life always talking at some stage or other. Sometimes I feel that by writing this narrative it becomes real, a series of scapegoats.

Piper down in the street, aeolian, insisting upon the immediate.

34   Funeral tomorrow. He telegraphs: *Long way back, wrong passageway, please forgive.* . . . They grant him six to eight to live, the freshman with the insensible orders.

She writes back: 'Give me Balkan snipers over this any day of the week.'

Which path I say. My words were vague (the androgyne). The body and its organs was central to the ritual work of ancient societies. I personify that benediction which the eclipsing curve of birth cannot quench.

35   He chooses the number seven, who signifies an emerald table. The less complicated option is infinity. The planchette scratched across the surface of a metal plate.

'I could then reconstruct exactly the method by which the diamond had been abstracted.'

He's clearly new to this job. In the adjoining room his lover lies in a trance. He refused. They tried hypnosis: he knew God as a hidden and at the same time supra-personal erection. She insisted; he still refused. I can no longer breathe the air they breathe. What lingers between us and the wall? And the eyes too are removed – you put them in a special place, where nobody will ever find them.

36   Distant crack of untimely brickbats. Here's today's challenge (the two pieces of music have been cleverly interwoven). I've just been walking along the seafront and I am totally blind. The other says dust particles; the correct answer is air.

The ninth letter of the Greek alphabet is transliterated as *i.*

37   I have to prove. I have to prove I am my only mother's son. The defeated army flees to the north. This whole unforeseen and tragic tale had made him speak ten times over on the way back.

'Her father has invented a new kind of pipe. He had all these windows. . . .'

My, doesn't it look funny seeing people walking around over there, wailing.

38   Shard-heap in desert, blockage at left lung, acute pain – voiceless alveolar stops, shorthand radio. They tore out his tongue and sheared off his left hand, the more useful of the two. It was feudal. If the alembic shatters, his blood will spread across the floor and you will not have anything left to bargain with. Consequently, there were two persons in him, the person assuming and the person assumed.

39   Dull ache below rib cage. Hour upon hour the ration of air, inhaled beyond certainty. The hub drops out. If I can only find the long walk, I shall recite the reading and thank all present. The location of the pin signals an armed location you must travel to. Things happen, don't they.

'The mechanism is a receptacle for capturing and storing. Wait for me.'

This creature had a spring-loaded retina.

40   Blood is the obvious. Your job is apparent undone. We must burrow into our own epoch, see if it translates into something useful at the skeletal level.

She's now famous for being a victim, all sorts of shapes, infinite patterns of torment – brink of hole, no shilly-shally before the end. We are about to be torn through the mill; I love this place. What fresh souls to bring in before the transference window closes?

No better authority could be imagined for a ghost story.

41   He is attempting to sell a used anecdote. The remaining branches are decaying. Coptic is now extinct she says. Who could be more suited than I to set the public record straight.

'So what's your plan.'

The advert contains some of the symbols needed to cope, i.e. a kind of trap.

'Child, child, I am repeat myself. . . .'

This suggests a person licenced to teach in a mediaeval university.

42   It rotates thus, the plane of polar light, beam swung out from the old liver-switch – note the Martello tower, flickering Super 8. The country you discovered strikes me as enormously pig. True schizophrenics lack the superego element present in paranoia.

'Up, Pockets!'

This is comparable to a pit-stop. The surrounding nations behave like narrow border regions – he is horrified, pirated. He cannot learn to use words exactly as a normal person does. (Gin and germ-cake solve everything.) Is this the same man of whom we were once a part – he who is paid, yet refuses to task? He is back-formation, from salvage. That must have been worth seeing.

Sound of one-head clapping, dog panting. Bunk supine.

43   I'm just watching this. We don't have far to go. It's on the increase. I've been away for a few years, leaching hope.

44   He had a reputation for short stays. Beyond the boundary marker I glimpsed an array of erections. (We had gone in search of her father's arse.) My own descent was broken by a sonic net.

If I run downhill I lose all my moments; it's a catch twenty-two situation. One cannot listen to both options at once.

Approach control is come dawn. I wrote the message to F, which is encrypted in document C ZO #2. The code has to be scrambled beyond recall.

45   He arrives carrying a large green sack over one shoulder, her with asthmatic lapdog – arm in a basket, feather the iris. There are four newcomers here, parent.

Matt-black jets strafe the pebble beach. I don't get paid for nothing, porous information.

46   Distant lights. The good burghers drag in massive boulders and deposit them haphazardly along the crust of the sea. I was sentenced to three-and-a-half minutes (you'll have to make do with unbroken news today). Folk tried to shade that delicate head, skull fragile as burnt eggshell.

'How can you see where the line is, or the muzzle, or the crown of which you speak?'

There was no incentive to go forth and die.

'What do you want down here?' I asked.

The barkeep looked toward the men's room, and the drinker nodded.

47   I thought you had stroke. The sense has now passed over to the other side – taxes too on lees of wine, blue with vomitings, a bouquet of burnt copper and those metal-green flies.

'You know where the grain store is boy, the silo?'

We are in place of. She is bruised, he bloodied. A third of the way to the molten core, and we're still making good time. What is he waiting for, eyeing those leftovers?

He has been adding her up, secreting: hairless, orange-pink with glistening cerise interior.

48   Masses swarming everywhere, spectacularly bored of owning and waiting. Their spiny skin can be used as food, but some parts become highly toxic when threatened.

49   Count noun in Africa. A mental covering spread over a horse. The future rests upon a single notion that will not reach its fruition until after the armistice.

50   His remaining eye blurs. Our next station is a form of badland tenure, yet we're making good time. The judge urged his beast forward.
     He knows; I could weep. The egg white suddenly crystallizes.
     'You're doing it too. Stop now.'

51   He carries with him everywhere a large velvet duck (we're putting as much pressure on people as we can). Remotely they trigger the spring sunk into his back – things are dropping from his open throat and onto the track.
     It's said he yet speaks, the flesh part of an indispensable. I've given in to you – there's too much foliage, yet we can see nearby where he is hid; it's a miracle. Dispatch your adversary – keep strictly within the limits of a notional taste, don't sacrifice any of those fragile nerves.

52   Do they vinyl? Other countries were found to have no twilight at all. A magic feather – which he can manifest at any moment for protection – is introduced into the narrative: a flightless bird, fast-running, whose tail-barbs resemble. In an alley near the river I retrieved the spirit of John Dee.

53   A suture. The giant strides made by two bodies.
     I can think of nowhere I would rather be. It's always worth checking. Today every detail appears contaminated.
     A tree or shrub with large waxy flowers, or thereabouts.

54   Dog panting.
     Salpinx.
     An early hook for pulling off a horse.
     I lost all three of you in that ravine.

55   There's a pistol at the bottom of his canvas bag – it glistens in the moonlight, as if jewelled or flecked with glass, splinters of mirror. Other objects include a bone stripped of flesh.
     'What is he doing. What has he done.'

This recipe takes two hours. I decide to keep the cursed gift. I think about making a pencil sketch of the scene, then immediately change my mind. This feeds the option: a cracked, chalk-white town with rivulets of rust, and thus encores my misery by my folly.

56   The sea was phosphorescent, seeds of light kindled by the oarsman's stroke. He has now locked himself in his quarters, writing.

57   A woman hands me a box with clouds and a painted sky. The aforementioned city was once China. I feel nauseous. The words are all wishing words. Still very poor, I journey there: carriages at midnight were pledged.

Who can be blind to the point of not seeing that our will has nothing to do with our actions? We lost three of our companions on route.

58   Inside is a black ribbon bound to an invitation card. On the floor is a bar of soap bearing an address and a telephone number; the nearest galaxy is the Magellanic. And so ended the most disastrous war in the long course of history.

59   This is the promissory new start (it's all down to experience, not the psyche). She stopped me in the road.

When we arrive at the agreed rendezvous, there's nothing, just an empty space between two buildings. Hurrying past is a young man with an ashplant. His left hand, as though paralysed, lies flat on his chest. Upon the ground – this is more like it – the membranes that once joined tentacles to ribcage. The retina has detached; cannibalism is in the air. I've ringed the thumb whirls with red ink, in case transmission scars the imprint.

He receives a good beating for this (said bat). He's hung upside down from a metal hook; it was like an abattoir. Sovereignty is exclusion.

And furthermore, he tells me there is a yellow plaque whereby his son met an accident with fate.

Evidently the truce no longer has any meaning. Disruption was caused by what the company calls 'migrant inertia', a magnificent oxymoron. A number of species are red or yellow, or marked with white spots and stripes. Size varies considerably; there are four rows of sharpened teeth. I could hear the lift ascending.

No, this is me, there can be no doubt; I don't undertake such things lightly. I have not broken my fast. Silence and withdrawal are now revolutionary postures.

60 *A man lying on a bed tapping out Morse code, to confirm that he is still in the room.*

'Have I infected your transit?'

Without warning, he loses a wing and is hobbled for life. A man passes carrying an arm. This suggests an extremely small amount (compare with jot).

61 Citizens local, siphoning fuel. I forgot his name. Estuarine and freshwater deposits are best exemplified. The song on the jukebox was about Ava Gardner (the killers, junction be, the night of the iguana). . . . Breeze-block structures are thrown up to surround us – I'm reminded of the extramural charnel-pits of mediaeval Paris.

I sat on a terrace all day drinking beer in the sun – which does not mean that to destroy is to create, but that destruction is in itself an absolute value. Suddenly they burst in. It was agricultural. On all sides of me clicked meters and dials, and an instrument for measuring time by the stealing of water. I've lost that generational thing.

62 You were lucky. I have done my fit of wandering, the accursed share. The central glass glows with data.

VOICE: 'Do you know what this instrument does?' (A cylindrical thing of concrete.)

63 I have been sitting here for hours and nothing has changed. He perches himself on one of three stools facing the control panel. A parley – an improvised conference – takes place between the two sides. The talk is unnecessary and at length. Origin came early from obsolete, from saddlecloth, from hood.

'They just repeated over and over, until.' [*Drums on the zinc table top.*]

'I am foreblinded.'

The extent of rupture is gauged by the rejection of transcendence. The others are just barking out the cards.

64   An ashtray: correct. An uncertain lament. Everything seems futile. And a wall of windmills, hence the name which attaches itself to this part of the island (dog). I think that's enough for the time being.

Then the locals do that thing with a spare atom at full cock. She whispers something about the collider hidden beneath the earth.

'Whatever they do to me, I shall wait for you.'

65   You just have to remember to listen, and never trust anyone. After only six days, the patrol returns. We decided to change course and entered the road to F, pitching camp before dusk. The infrared out in space reveals clusters of hut circles invisible to the naked eye; our adversary is no longer in a more elevated position.

66   She's confined. Now she can't be bled or shot at – no more sanguinary nights. She harbours a tension. Cartridges are distributed and the guard alerted; no one suspects the significance of this drill, clumsily worked into the plot. For example, do they speak while carrying out these actions?

67   We have sundered the element – ironing was done, the ceiling polished. The ninth star in the constellation is *Iota Piscium*. Where are we going nowhere he said.

68   He settles wherever he finds himself. He has fond memories of the rows of a year past. (You'd be horrified.) They didn't even ask us how we got here – all day it was the collapsed, the dead. In a photograph on the dust cover the author looks benignly belligerent. The probe was deliberately burned up in the atmosphere of Venus.

69   I walk. I hail a hansom. I suffer the promised audience with the consul. I'm not moving again. We slide headlong into a ravine. We all perish.

70   Clear blue for sky tomorrows. . . . Let's make our way back: fuckwittage, chiromancy, spontaneous ignition – black magic, then renewal. I was rented, sex for pelf (those were the days). This is where the objective conditions of historical consciousness are reunited.

71   The wave passed. It seemed to me that I was under water for several minutes (really it was seconds). I looked forward. The blast had torn out the great sail – we mapped the surface using radar to penetrate the dense cloud cover.

72   He had a roaming eye. He was Irish. I needed a crash course. Life was interesting – it was all about. It escaped. High in the air, rags fluttered to leeward; from the crow's-nest, I had failed to catch sight of anything. Look at that gathering crowd.

You're searching for meaning where there is none. At this point we oblige by transforming repetition into a sequence of memories.

Now they're advertising the cyclone vacuum, an iron basket for combustibles, placed in a beacon, lighthouse or wharf – a small pit or hollow, in particular. Any of the tiny air sacs of the lung – bony socket for the root – scar-like gravity trapped in a gland. . . . I keep forgetting. (It's all lovely, everything's lovely.) And they can see it, they can see it – the names repeat themselves – the names are always the same.

Aplomb & Venom.

73   *Even while she gazed up at the mass, at the line, at the colour.*

She was poor, moreover, degradingly poor. When they ask why did grandmother leave the adjacent island, I answer hunger. There's been no drop in the wind speed at the racetrack. After work I felt sticky (i.e. beyond the walls, connected with a university but not under its direct control).

74   *Extranet. A torch, generally.*

A kerosene lamp swings from the rafters. We are back at that cabin in the woods. It has begun to snow. This may be a lost cause. Two diffuse luminous patches appear in the southern sky.

75   Mackerel front moving in, funnelling the prospect. Lots of changes in our tactics have been augured. We are trekking west through a snowscape, a trail of covered wagons, shreds of carbon on a white field.

Origin in a sense, a talk between people and their traders – from word, from comparison (see parabola).

Many of our number perished.

76   She's slow and steady; he'll get jealous. I made some calls – a constant, low-level murmur of conversation, seemingly from inside my own head (the amygdala). Fingers crossed, the counsel.

It's surprisingly easy, a good day to be under sail. She was lean and sinewy, brittle. The night is so dark there's not a star to be seen in the whole sky.

Child with toy, makeshift, with helium rictus.

The Brain

Toby Olson

Because of an awkward splashing, brought on by an urgency that had recently come to plague him, Roger found it necessary to sit down while urinating, and in time he found this posture quite pleasing, those brief moments of contemplation.

The toilet was in the far corner of the basement, and he rushed away from the work table where he had been dealing with the old lamp he had only recently acquired, holding himself until he reached the throne.

He'd purchased the lamp at a second hand shop in the town center. It was an elegant thing, a tall hollow pewter cylinder above which a gathering of glass tulips, each fitted with a small white light, sprayed out in ascending circles, topped with a pewter finial shaped like a tulip bud. He had carefully placed the lamp on its side when the toilet called, and then, back at the table again, he adjusted the swing arm lamp and, removing the felt covering at the base, peered into the hollow tube, seeing that someone had replaced wires in a crude and thoughtless way.

The old wires had been clipped only five inches from their source, new wires clumsily taped to them. A real fire hazard, he thought. He'd have to rewire the whole thing, something he looked forward to with pleasure.

For over a year Roger had been on permanent disability. No more work at the shoe factory, where he had come to notice a gradual change in production. Military boots had become the order of the day, lows and highs with visible steel toes and small devices imbedded in their heels. And in his free time, which was almost all of the time now, he'd taken to shopping, mostly in secondhand and consignment shops, but also for clothing, groceries, and whatever else caught his fancy. He bought things, mostly electrical for fiddling, but he had also come to enjoy browsing, moving in and out of shops in the town center and at the large mall that had grown up on the edge of the highway. And books. He'd never been much of a reader before his accident, but in the last year he'd begun what he thought might end up as a not insignificant little library. History and art books, how-to electrical tomes, and even a few novels, mostly of romance, but some of foreign intrigue that argued for political change. He'd come across a book called *The Feminine Mystique* . It was there on the new bookcase he'd built in the living room. He seemed to remember the book somehow, though he had not as yet read it.

He had reached up into the bowels of the lamp, aiming to pull the frayed tape away, when the lights went out, the basement thrust into darkness.

A breaker, he thought. He knew the basement well, and without pausing to get his bearings, he headed for the small enclosure beside the stairs where the breaker box was located. He had a small light, together with a few pencils and pens, tucked into a plastic container that was, in turn, tucked into his shirt pocket, and he shined the narrow beam into the box, seeing that nothing had tripped. Puzzled, he stood there for a moment, considering. Then he turned and shined the little light on the main switch. It had not been thrown.

He stood very still, there in the darkness, listening, feeling silly, and suddenly the lights came back on. He could hear nothing, but he noticed a faint scent that seemed unfamiliar. Could it be sweat? A thing distantly burning? He shook it off. Something with that dammed electric company again. This had happened before, and he'd called numerous times, only to be put on hold, then disconnected. He shook his head, adjusted his wig, and went back to his electrical work.

He had awakened in a fog of misunderstanding. His vision was hazy, and he could not hear with clarity. He thought he was in bed, coming back from a troubling dream. But then he felt the tube in his nose, saw the vague bag of solution hanging from the IV pole. Figures surrounded him, nurses he suddenly realized. I'm in the hospital. What happened?

"An accident." A whispered voice. He must have spoken his last thought. "In the factory." Then he remembered bits of it: the toe lasting machine, hot glue. He'd known the uppers on the boots were too thick. Was he burning? He didn't feel any burns. He had a headache. "We can't give you anything for the pain just yet." That soft, soothing voice again. "The doctor will be here soon." Then he drifted back into sleep.

He awakened to the sight of a small, chubby man with a mustache leaning over him.

"I'm the doctor," the man said. "Can you hear me?"

"Some," Roger said. "Enough maybe."

"Well," the doctor said. "At least there's that."

"At least?" Roger said, or thought he said.

"Yes," the doctor replied. "And I have news, and it's upsetting and rather urgent."

Roger didn't understand. "I can't see too well. I have a bad headache."

"To be expected," the doctor said. "But we can fix all that. We do have to hurry though."

"With what?" Roger asked.

"The transplant."

"What do you men?" Roger said. "I don't understand."

"Well," the doctor said. "Let me explain."

He had been wearing a helmet, as required, when the toe lasting machine failed, and hot glue had washed over the leather, then found the portal and flooded into his left ear.

"What it did was a little like cooking. I mean it cooked a good portion of your brain. And it is still in there, drying, and doing it's dirty work, sealing, rendering further matter quite useless. We need to operate, and we need to do it quickly. Now I know you have insurance, but it won't cover the transplant, unless..."

"What transplant?"

"Your brain, man! We have to replace your brain!"

"You can't do that."

"Indeed we can. But there are options. Decisions. Forms to be filled out."

"And if I don't agree to this?"

"Then I'm afraid you're finished. Soon to be dead."

"What are the options?" Roger said

"There are two. In our tissue bank we have a dozen or so male brains. These are somewhat costly and difficult to install. And I doubt that insurance would cover the operation. The brains themselves are expensive, as is the operation."

"How expensive?" Roger asked.

"Sixty-five thousand dollars each, plus around twenty for the procedure."

"My God! That's a fortune! I can't afford that. What did you mean by each?"

"Each male brain."

"But I'd only need one, wouldn't I?"

"Well, of course. Just one."

"You said two. What's the other option?"

"Well, there are the female brains. A few, about four, are available as we speak. And in this case the operation would be covered by virtue of a grant. We're studying them. The fit can be awkward. Different skull configurations after all."

"How much?"

"Fifteen thousand. A flat rate. No hidden costs."

"Why?" Roger asked.

"Why what?"

"Why are the female brains so much cheaper than the male ones?"

"Well," the doctor answered, They've been used."

"Used? Like a used car?"

"Sure. A metaphor. Something like that. Though maybe 'broken in' would be more accurate. And there is no warranty. You'd be taking your chances."

And so he took his chances, and the brain, that of a thirty-five year old woman, was installed. The fit was a tight one, and even after some necessary adjustments, Roger's eyes were slightly to the side of their sockets, giving him a rakishly provocative glance. So too had their been difficulties with the new brain's neural pathways, his getting used to them. It was almost as if he were two perceivers now, or at least had come to understand the world around him differently than he had before. Was there awareness somewhere in his body in addition to that in his new brain, something at the base of his spine, himself in his motor responses, something seated elsewhere?

Was he a woman now? The doctor had scoffed at that idea as he'd handed over the Geniux, a brain pill championed by Dr. Oz. "This might help with concentration. It's like Viagra for the brain."

At first all this was quite unsettling, but in only a brief time he had grown accustomed to a kind of double-vision. He began to feel integrated, though his hair had not grown back, and once up and around he had selected a wig that held waves and curls and a brush of hair that drifted over his left ear. Roger was fifty-five years old, but he felt much younger once the surgery and his recuperation were behind him.

Now he continued work on the new lamp, and while doing so he thought back on his visit to the second-hand shop where he had purchased it.

He was shocked as always, though less so since the operation, when he stepped beyond the front door of his house. The street was gone, as were the familiar houses that had faced his across from it. There was rubble still, both straight ahead and to the right, acres of it, and the only familiarity resided in the beginning of the forest that abutted his lawn to the left. Men had come to visit him, dressed in suits that seemed vaguely military. They had made offers, not very good ones, though he knew his neighbors had cashed in for much less. He might have sold had the suits come up with something substantial. They hadn't though.

He was at the very edge of the construction site, and it was clear that they could build what they wanted without his land getting in the way. At least for a while. He'd tried to learn what the project was all about. He gone to city hall to look at the plans, but none were available for viewing. The clerk had been sheepish, and when he went back and tried again, there was a different clerk, a stern woman dressed like the men who had visited him, who dismissed him and his enquiry immediately. "This is a government project," she'd said. "Nothing is available to be viewed by the populace." Her language was formal and strict, a little arcane, and he left with nothing at all.

He made his way across the empty acreage, coming to places where the ground had been leveled and cleared, where there was new curbing and cuts through brush in preparation for roads, and finally stepped onto pavement where the edge of the town began. It was late-afternoon, and cloudy, and lights had been turned on in the various shops he passed by. On the door of each house and each shop, a small, sturdy metal box had been affixed, a series of buttons on each of them. Codes to be punched in. But by whom? New street lights stood, every thirty or so yards along the curbing, and each sported an elaborate surveillance camera beside its hooded canopy. He heard a vague clicking as they turned to track his progress. He thought he heard the chop of a helicopter in the quickly darkening sky.

When he stepped into the dimly lit store, he saw that there were only a few shoppers milling around. The owner, who seemed somewhat tense, was standing stiffly behind the counter. Roger was focused on the section that held the lamps but suddenly felt a little faint and gripped the edge of the counter to right himself. Beside his focused, pragmatic concentration, there was a more generalized awareness now. He could feel it behind his forehead and knew it in his eyes as they began to dilate even though nothing in the room's dim lighting had changed. It's you, he thought. It's me. His focus broadened, opening out as his head lifted, and then. . . she was taking in the entire space, its feel and its gestalt. There was something ominous, an atmosphere she thought she would come to understand, but not yet. She scanned the room, slowly, the book shelves, the counters of electrical gear, the few people present, the nature of the dim lighting. Most of the books were light reading: mysteries, self-help, a number of large coffee-table tomes. But there was something, a thin spine, Sun Tzu's *The Art of War.* What was it doing here? Why were the shoppers not looking to buy anything? They were just watching, gazing out the broad street-side windows, studying those passing by. They seemed to be waiting for something.

Roger had focused on the book she had drawn his attention to, but she had passed beyond it and was now staring at the man who had emerged from the bathroom behind the counter and was speaking intently to the store owner as his machine ground out a key. He was a tall, thick man, dressed in a outfit reminiscent of military garb. His jaw seemed slack, his thin lipped mouth half open in dumb show, as he listened to the owner who then handed him the key.

Roger felt the skin on his face tighten, his eyes watering. He had recognized the shoes. My husband, she thought, the bastard, right here, right now. He can't see me, but I can see him. Soon, she thought. Roger lifted the lamp and moved to the counter. He nodded to the owner. Now he could smell the other, something rancid behind the scent of alcohol and cigarettes. He looked away from the owner, who was ringing up his purchase, gazed into the face of the other. Not one of the three smiled.

After a late dinner consisting of broiled lamb chops dredged in a little olive oil then rubbed lightly with herb de provence and salt and pepper, this accompanied by sauteed asparagus spears and new potatoes baked in oil, garlic and ginger sticks, Roger settled into his easy chair in the living room, a cup of fresh ground coffee and the morning's constructed crème brulée in a custard dish on the table beside him, and read his paper.

Twice more the lights had gone out, then, in a brief while, had come back on. There seemed no reason to call. He knew he wouldn't get through. He spent these times in darkness, poised at the table, or sitting still with his paper in his lap.

He had taken up cooking since his transplant. Before that it had been TV dinners and various canned meats. Then he had discovered a complete Julia Child boxed set in one of his travels to a second hand book store in the mall. He'd bought it, read it, and then embarked on what he thought of as a wonderful journey. I might become a cook, he'd thought, and so he had.

There was a good deal in the paper these days, much of it having to do with the new president and his accomplishments. He was a tall, handsome man, at least he liked to think of himself that way. But the campaign had taken its toll, his blond hair had thinned and turned grey, and a new softness had replaced muscle in his shoulders and hips. Even his behind now sagged in his finely tailored clothing, and his mouth was often pursed in an unattractive way, as it was in the photograph Roger was gazing at, one in which the president stood in front of a construction site, a large sign held up by some rough looking men behind him. *America Has Been Made Great Again* the sign pronounced, somewhat awkwardly.

Very little had been made great, at least on the international front, as promised, in his first two years in office -the second year of his reign, Roger thought-, but domestically much had been done, most of it having to do with security and surveillance: fear of the immigrant population, drug addicts, and domestic terrorists. Even in Roger's little town, the results of presidential edicts were in evidence. Cameras everywhere, chips installed, often against individual wishes, in cars, shoes, phones, and even in houses and workplaces when just the vaguest of suspicion was aroused.

And Roger knew this was only the beginning, for now the president had put forward his supreme court nominee, one to fill a vacancy in that august, though currently divided, body.

Alfred Bub Hawkins, known in his southern district as Big Bub, was a former mid-level official in the Ku Klux Klan. He had earned his law degree at a small Christian college, scoring 10th in a class of 12, then had gone to work in his home town, his practice consisting mostly of writing up contracts and notarizing documents, with a few divorce cases thrown in for good measure.

He was no great shakes. But he could write. He'd published a bevy of articles, all dealing with constitutional interpretation and its application regarding both central government powers and states rights. His articles were deemed brilliant, at least by those in the president's coterie and the members of the senate that had been investigated and found culpable enough to be bent to his will. Yet it was rumored that it was Hawkins' wife who had written the articles for him.

Alma Hawkins was an uneducated housewife who liked to read. She had studied the Constitution and the Supreme Court opinions, both majority and dissenting, in great detail, until she had come close to memorizing them in the way some had memorized the bible. She had also memorized the Bible and could quote it word for word, both the Old and New Testaments.

Roger had read the paper straight through. A few local arrests that seemed oddly unnecessary, some jargon about government construction projects, nothing at all of an international appeal. Still, he read on, his only interest piqued by the fashion section, new clothing, mostly for women, that seemed retrograde, very little for men there.

He'd finished his days work on the new lamp, had carefully cleaned the small glass tulips that contained the miniature bulbs, a few of which had burned out and would need replacing. He'd have to shop for those, but that would come in a day or two. Now he was tired, though not exhausted, and decided he'd go up to bed and read a little before sleep. His bedroom was on the third floor, which was no more than an attic that he had refitted as a small study and bedroom. He liked the isolation, the cosiness of the space, and felt oddly protected there, though why he needed protection was beyond him.

He had settled between the sheets in a seated posture, then reached for the chain on his bedside lamp. Nothing. A bulb, he thought, but when he felt for it, it was not there. How can this be? he thought. What the devil is going on? He rose from the bed and put on his robe, then moved through both the bedroom and his study, searching for any evidence that someone had been there. He could find nothing amiss. Tomorrow, he thought. I'll check the entire house. Then he went to the small storage closet where he kept his paper, pencils and pens and removed a new bulb from its sleeve. He returned to the bedroom then and screwed it in.

Back under the covers again, he reached for the book he was currently reading, *Our Bodies, Ourselves*, the chapter on violence against women. He managed to get through only a couple of pages before his lids were falling. Enough, he thought. Later. Then he pulled the lamp's chain, turned on his side, and in only a few moments was fast asleep.

Somewhere in the early morning hours, he had a dream that was not a dream but a gathering of memories that he had no recollection of when he awoke.

Early morning. Still dark. Could have been the salad, or the wine. Probably the salad. There are cracks in the ceiling. The cheap tulips he had brought, white, teardrop buds in the night light's soft gleam. The high pole with its miserable camera and flood. She could see it only vaguely through the open window, the curtains lifting in the soft, chemical breeze.

His smiling close attention to her needs. He had chattered across the table. Even candles. She can't move. She can move. But only her head. She's in the bed. Figures swaying in the room, furniture and shadows.

He had bent down over her, still smiling: "Are you happy now? I'll get what I want."

They had been married for six long years, and he had made the conscious choice, at the very beginning, to drift away from her, until she knew—his way of addressing her, a gradual hardening in his eyes, his distance in sex—that it was the money. Which was really very little, thirty thousand dollars from the sale of her deceased parents' house.

In the past year he had beaten her, pounding her in the ribs and kidneys, those thirty thousand dollars in his eyes. He was strong, and he would hold her by the wrist as he punched her. Through it all she remained stoic, at least she seemed so. She went to work at the coffee shop. She didn't socialize. She read books. And when she wasn't working, or reading, or cleaning, or fixing his meals, she spent her time hating him, wishing him dead.

He worked in construction, a small failing company of his own. Half a dozen men. Enough work to keep them alive, not much, though buildings were going up, and many were coming down to make room for the new. All this under a perpetual layer of smog and construction dust that blackened the town and its environs, causing the populace to move about in medical masks, their hair under their caps greasy and their faces and eyelids blackened. And he was looking for the big job, something to get him back on his feet again, and he'd told her he'd found something and was aiming to get it. And he'd told her that he loved her, repeatedly, after he'd beaten her. That smile. The obvious lie.

That evening, after the dinner and candles and wine, he'd left her. Put her into the bed. There was a meeting of his crew, he'd said. Discussion of the new jail that would replace the high school basement as the temporary venue for incarceration of those who were seen to defy, in any way at all, the new order. He had a small part in it, curbing and a sidewalk. She knew there would be drinking, possibly drugs, and women.

Fragments and regrets. Her eyes were alive. Her head seemed to be dying. She was tired. She needed sleep. She fell asleep. Ten empty minutes.

And when she awoke she couldn't awake. She was awake, but only in her eyes. Fading cracks in the ceiling. Insubstantial shadows. I'm going away, she thought. Nightshade. She went away.

Roger awoke in earthquake. His bed was shaking, and when he sat up he saw that the whole room was rocking. He felt he was in a topsy-turvy fun house. His lamp teetered, then fell from the table and bounced on the floor. He rose quickly, hearing a pounding down below, and slipped into his bathrobe, a lacy satin number that he had purchased in a small boutique at the mall. His wig, too quickly pulled on, had slipped down onto his forehead, and his slippers were on the wrong feet. The pounding continued, and he rushed down the stairs. It was the front door, shifting on its hinges. He opened it to find a small man in uniform, four large earth moving monstrosities, digging and banging their yellow scoops on the ground near his foundation. The man raised his arm and waved it above his head. The activity stopped, the machines belching and sighing into silence behind him. And in that silence the man spoke.

"What? What!," Roger said, his ears ringing.

"It's time we spoke," the man said, smirking, gazing at Roger's headgear and his strange attire, and they did, or rather the man spoke, and Roger listened.

They wanted his house, and they aimed to get it. The previous offer was no longer in place. Now it was twice that. The little man sat in the couch, he feet tap-tapping on the floor.

"Have you been having any problems, with your electricity?" He asked this in an odd, conspiratorial fashion.

Roger didn't answer.

"I have the papers here. And the check." He produced them from the thin briefcase he clutched a his side.

It was a lot of money, and though Roger wished only to drive the little prick out of his house, he swallowed his pride. He was surrounded by construction, noise and filth, and now the deal with the electricity.

"I have to think about it," he said.

"Yes, you do. But don't take too long."

"I won't. But now. How about leaving me alone."

The little man seemed about to speak, to bring forth further insinuations, but then he saw the look in Roger's eyes, nodded and left the house.

It was after dinner than evening, something light, a fillet of flounder, thinly breaded and coated with herbs, then pan fried in butter, when Roger thought he heard something down in the basement. Actually it was she who heard it first, then rocked their brain slightly to the side until Roger too caught it. I know who it is, she thought, his scent.

Roger rose from the table and went to the basement door, then climbed down the stairs.

The man was there, the one Roger had seen talking to the owner at the store. He seemed to be studying the walls. A heavy wooden beam ran across the basement ceiling, from outer wall to outer wall. It was supported by a couple of lally columns and hung low into the basement. Even Roger, who was only five ten, had to duck slightly so as not to hit his head, and when the man turned, hearing Roger's approach, he had to bend down considerably. He did so, then came up smiling and extended his hand. Roger didn't take it.

"What exactly are you doing here. How did you get in?"

He was dressed in some sort of uniform, a breast patch, hard to read, identifying him as working for the government, Roger thought.

"Well, you see, I was sent in to check for any illegal devices. And the electrical." A sheepish smile followed this last statement, reaching for irony that wasn't there.

"It's nothing, just routine. I have a key." He held it out as a child might have, smiling as he showed his prize.

"But more to the point, I think I've got the contract to tear this place down. Not yet, of course. Not until the sale is completed. Will it be completed soon? I just wanted to have a look."

He was grinning then. Nothing snide, or conspiratorial. Just a grinning from and into a certain emptiness. Something wrong and primitively evil, Roger thought. It's him, she thought.

The man stared into his eyes as Roger moved closer, and when he was just inches from him, looking up, he saw her eyes where his had been.

"My God, I don't understand," he said, his voice squeaking. And that was the last thing he ever said.

Roger leaped up and rammed his forehead into the man's startled face, and as he fell he hit him again, this time skull to skull. There was a sharp cracking, a rush of blood. He was dead then, sprawled out on the basement floor, and Roger smiled, or she smiled. And it was done.

They painted a section of the beam with his blood. Then they called the police, who came, a half dozen of them, almost immediately. Each wore a large breast patch that read *America's Great Again.*

He'd heard a sharp whack from the basement while he was eating dinner, then found the man, bloody and broken, on the basement floor. He must have hit his head against the low beam. The police seem to know that he was there. They asked Roger if he intended to sell the place, and he replied in the affirmative. Each shook his hand. The ambulance came, and they took the body away. There would be no further investigation.

Later that night, Roger placed two large pillows, end to end, in the bed beside him. Then, once the covers were pulled up over him, he lay on his side, snuggled up, spoon fashion, against them. One tucked in against his stomach and groin, the other, hugged close, rested against his cheek. He breathed in the smell of eucalyptus, the scent she had used most frequently throughout her too short life. It was quiet now, no construction, no helicopters, no sirens.

"Did you mind very much killing him?"

"I didn't. You did."

"Well, I guess you're right. The instrument. But the intention."

"Did *you* mind it?"

"Yes and no. Mostly no."

"Well, at least America's Great Again."

"And will you really sell this place? Will you move away?"

"Yes. I've decided. Out of this town. Into the country."

"Where it is quiet."

"Yes."

"Can I come with you?"

"Well, of course. There is no alternative"

"Good."

"We'll dress well in bib overalls, a blue cotton work shirt, pearl buttons."

"And a straw hat, with a bright red ribbon around the crown."

"A little garden. Herbs and fine greens."

"I like to cook."

"And in the evenings, a good brandy. Books. A little TV."

"Then off to bed."

"I'm tired. It's been a busy day."

"But what about cakes and pies? Ice cream and custard?"

"All that as well. Anything we like."

"I can bake. I'm good at that."

"And I can help."

"No two have ever been this close.

"As one."

"But, boy, am I tired! A long busy day."

"Well then."

"Goodnight."

"Night. Sweet Dreams."

Things That Try to Happen

Michael Upchurch

A received idea is not a living idea.

From the moment I moved into this house, I felt I'd been given a blank canvas to work with. The floor-plan was straightforward. The living room was on the right, with the bedroom just beyond it. The dining room lay on the left, with kitchen directly adjoining. The bathroom was off in the corner, its plumbing back-to-back with that of the kitchen sink and dishwasher.

Serviceable as this structure was, I felt the need to tamper with it. I imagined voids where there were walls. I imagined skies where there were ceilings. Most of all I felt the house calling to me, asking me to change its essence, suggesting ways I could speed up its fate, badgering me to make things happen that were trying to happen.

I was reluctant to do so, however, until I had witnesses.

To that end, I hosted a barbecue for my neighbors on either side of me.

I. MEAT AND GREET

Turkey sausage, tofu burgers, salmon fillets, a small pork loin—I wanted to offer something for every taste. And sure enough, this worked. As aromatic smoke trailed out into the street, my neighbors emerged from their houses, eager to follow these scents to their source.

To my north lived a couple, Nathan and Melanie, who were a contrast in types. Nate—heavy-set, slow-moving, firm in his handshake—was a contractor who worked for himself, restoring and remodeling old houses. Melanie, a beautician with long and lustrous golden hair, was as hyper as her husband was sedate. She greeted me cheerily, before turning toward the grill to see if she could take charge: "Do these need to be turned, you think?"

To my south lived a slightly younger couple: Vincent and Violetta.

They gave off a measured cool where Nate and Melanie gave off only social anxiety. Vincent was handsome, slender, mercurial, turning every phrase he spoke into sly self-deprecation. He seemed a golden boy whose possibilities were more theoretical than actual.

Violetta, by contrast, was fully realized, satisfyingly complete. Her languid gaze was knowing and alert. Whenever she gave her name, even in its most abbreviated form, she stretched out every possible syllable: "Vi … ee … ee."

All four wanted a house tour, so I led them through my five small rooms. They inspected the stove in the kitchen, the tile-work around the bathtub, the rheostat in the dining room and the fireplace in the living room. Then they spent an unusually long time in the bedroom, where there was only a rumpled mattress on the floor.

"That's a nice touch," Violetta said in her husky Peruvian accent, waving her hand at a detail so vague it seemed to encompass the whole room.

"What is?" I asked.

She lifted her eyes up toward the peeling cracks in the stucco ceiling.

"Came with the house," I told her.

"You got big plans?" Nate asked, eyeing the messy mattress as if that were the first thing he'd deal with.

"Not really," I said. "I want to get the feel of the place first. Take it a day at a time."

Melanie fretted: "No one's watching the grill!"

We scooted back out to the yard, where the barbecue was done. Wines were brought out. A salad was made. The evening grew blurry.

In saying our goodbyes an hour or so later, the cordial handshakes of earlier in the evening turned to light social kisses and warm enveloping hugs—or, in Vi's case, a triple buss on the cheeks, presumably of Latin American origin.

We promised to get together soon—very soon.

Once I'd done a little more work on the place.

II. Maximum Appreciation of the Minimum Change

When you're a bachelor you can do things with a dining room that you could never do if you had a partner to consult.

You can purchase two gallons of yellow paint—one called "Citrus" and the other "Forsythia"—and experiment with various wall sections. You can see what a "Forsythia" hand-print looks like on a "Citrus" backdrop, and vice versa. You can even lay newspapers down on the floor, strip off all your clothes and find out what a "Citrus" *body-print* looks like on a bright "Forsythia" background.

In the bathroom, you can trace an old lover's name in the grime of the tub, then observe how many showers it takes to wash it away.

In the kitchen, you can move the plates to where the glasses used to be and the glasses to where the plates once were.

Living-room changes can be identified upon request.

As for the bedroom, it's amazing how much of the sullied and the sordid you can imply there, without having to change a thing....

III. Not Why, But When

Nate and Mel seemed nervous the following week about what they might see—or might be *expected* to see—as I took them from one room to another. I said nothing. I offered no hint. I let them make whatever they wanted to make of it.

Melanie was the first to react: "Wow, when did you do all this?"

"All what?"

"I think it's fantastic," she rushed on. "I knew you must have something in mind, but I never—"

"Yeah, when did you find the time?" Nate inquired. "I thought you said—"

"Well, *I* think it's just darling!" Melanie jumped in. "And you've managed it all so quickly!"

Nate was less certain. Speaking from the dining room, with its barely distinguishable yellows covered in barely discernible handprints, he said, "You know, I have a house-painter friend. I could give you his number. Fix you up, if you like."

"No need, no need."

It seemed to me he was deliberately ignoring the full-frontal body impressions I'd made, flecked with chest hairs and public hairs. But I couldn't exactly fault him for this.

"Where's your broom?" Mel asked, eyeing the dust on the floor. "We should sweep that up for you."

"Seriously, don't worry."

She laughed dismissively, then skipped toward the kitchen to find some cleaning implements.

I had to get stern with her.

"Leave it, Mel. I mean it."

She dithered a little, still not taking me at my word—then caught the look in my eye, drew closer to her husband, and said, "Well, I guess we should go now."

"Yeah, it's getting late," Nate said.

I didn't contradict him.

"Nice seeing you," he added. "And if you ever need a hand—"

I gave him the firm send-off he evidently needed.

"Thanks—but I'm good."

IV. PARDON MY APPEARANCE—I'M UNDER CONSTRUCTION

Skin is a door. If you want to, you can open it.

Another fine thing about being a bachelor is that you can turn your bathroom into a darkroom, nailing a large sheet of plywood over the only window and installing a more powerful ventilation fan in the wall above—and no one is there to stop you or complain about it.

In the dark I was able to make more progress. My "Citrus" and "Forsythia" hand- and body-imprints on the dining room wall seemed like child's play now. It felt good to block all sunlight from the bathroom. It felt right to open "a breathing space" between bedroom and living room. I had always wanted to pick up a sledgehammer and slam it into someone's wall.

Now I had the chance. These walls, after all, were my walls.

My first swing, however, was so timid it embarrassed me.

You tell yourself you know what you're after. You convince yourself you're about to make a breakthrough. You aren't always sure what it takes to accomplish it. It's always more difficult than you'd think to discern how focused effort guides the flow of things just trying to happen.

My second swing was more powerful. I mustered my strength, put real muscle behind it—and wound up with the sledgehammer stuck in the drywall, its handle poking down at a slanting phallic angle.

It took some doing to dislodge it. But once I had, I was well on my way. I made the opening larger. I built up a sweat. I shrugged off layers of clothing until I was standing there naked. My muscles were sore with the effort. Perspiration dripped into my eyes.

My reward: A ragged three-foot opening soon spread out in front of me. Fiberglass insulation stood revealed. I had just started pulling it out when I heard Vince call from the front door, "Anyone home?"

"In here!"

As he entered the living room, he nodded toward the mess and wisecracked: "No need to ask when you did *that*. We've been hearing you at it all morning."

"Sorry to disturb you."

"Not at all, not at all," he said, as he looked me up and down.

"It's just that—well, you've whetted our curiosity."

Then, studying the battered drywall more closely, he asked, "I don't suppose I could take a bash?"

I handed him the sledgehammer: "Do your worst."

He followed roughly the same striptease trajectory I had, only in reverse. The first thing to go was his footwear. This seemed a canny move. There was something about being barefoot on a hardwood floor that channeled strength up through his legs and thighs and torso until it culminated in the surging swing of his sledgehammer into the ever-widening gap. With one satisfying blow after another, he hit the destructive sweet spot, expanding the hole to a point where it seemed no wall had ever been there. Soon he was stripped down, too, the sweat pouring off him. Exploding plaster-dust coated his damp skin in an almost tribal guise.

I got out my camera out and went to work on him.

V. DELICATELY ASSEMBLED AND STRUCTURALLY UNSOUND

All possibilities are perfect. Only in the realization do they acquire flaws.

Melanie, in slacks and high turtleneck, entered my partly demolished home as if eager to restore it to its original pristine condition. She fussed, she scrutinized, she tut-tut-tutted. She was entirely confident of her place here and utterly presumptive about her role in my scheme of things. It was almost as if Nate, as substantial as he was, weren't enough husband to keep her fully occupied.

"I could vacuum that up for you," she said, nodding toward the sediments of plaster rippling across the living-room floor.

"No need."

"Want me to run those through the laundry?" she asked, of the soiled bedsheets sprawling from my mattress.

"Please don't."

"These counters sure could use some scrubbing!" she sang from the kitchen. "And what's this in the sink?"

It was a reddish brown stain that didn't smell so good. Possibly mildew.

I asked her not to interfere, and she managed to restrain

herself.

As she darted from one corner of the house to the next, she did her best to ignore the gigantic nudes of Vincent that I'd taped to the walls. She exclaimed over the cobwebs hanging from the ceiling. She dragged her finger down a windowpane and said it could use a little Windex. She asked when I'd last run the dishwasher.

"If you don't run it regularly," she warned me, "it becomes less capable."

I did not ask: *Capable of what?*

In the meantime, the photographs of Vince were proving more and more distracting to her.

We aren't accustomed to seeing our neighbors in this light. Vincent, in my shots of him, was a sauntering Priapus, cock fully erect. He glanced toward her—as he had toward me—first from one angle, then from another, his gaze both gentle and incendiary.

"We need to get a cleaning service in here!" she fluttered. "Don't you think?"

She was in a tailspin, the hapless play-thing of her barely repressed desires—until, exhausted, she lost her momentum.

Only then did she take a longer look at these images of Vince in his various stages of arousal. After studying them for several minutes, she turned and asked, almost wearily, "So when did you take all *those*?"

"Last Thursday."

"Gosh," she said. "That recently...."

She seemed particularly drawn to the rear-shots that emphasized the spread of Vincent's shoulders, the tapering of his back and the downy double curve of his buttocks, leading your eye toward his equally downy thighs. I expected her to ask if this were a shrine of some sort or a declaration of illicit desire. Perhaps it was a prank he had put me up to or a prospective submission for an all-male skin magazine.

What she *did* say was: "I just don't know where you find the time. Between the beauty parlor and all my housework, I never have a moment to spare."

She scanned the room, maybe for a duster, maybe for an escape route.

Finding nothing, she wrapped her arms around herself as if to fend off any sexual interests on my part—or Vince's, for that matter—and headed for the door, the tightness of her turtleneck seeming to give her some protection she felt she still needed.

VI. THE BIRTH OF WRECKAGE

Was it a shrine I was building, or the desecration of a shrine?

In the most explicit photos of Vincent, the sheen at the tip of his cock matched a sheen at the corner of his smiling lips, as though something precious, or even holy, were about to filter into existence. Or was he simply about to come?

Nate was all business the next day after I called him in for a consultation. He turned up promptly at the appointed time and didn't bat an eye when I told him what I wanted.

Gaping holes in the walls, I had come to realize, were not enough for me. I needed *no* walls where there wasn't a need for walls. I needed to know which posts were load-bearing and which were dispensable.

"Wow!" he said as he walked in. "When did all this happen?"

"Last week," I answered.

Unlike his wife, he was frank in taking in the sight of bold priapic Vincent on the walls around him—or what little remained of those walls.

Then, shaking his head as though at a standard of masculine physique he knew he could never attain, he accompanied me into the kitchen and, pointing behind the sink and stove, said, "Now this I wouldn't mess with—at least not with a sledgehammer."

"Why not?"

"One wrong move and you'll either blow the place up or flood it."

"Fair enough. What about in here?"

I led him into the bathroom.

"Well, like I said, you're asking for trouble if you mess with the pipes. You could knock that one down—" He pointed to the wall abutting the bedroom. "—but that wouldn't give you much privacy when you shower or take a dump."

Slight pause.

"Unless," he ventured, "that's what you're after...?"

I answered by holding his gaze and making a mute query of

my own.

Flustered, he side-stepped this and continued: "Also, I see you're using this as your darkroom. If you want to keep doing that, you'd have to seal all the windows in your bedroom. I can't make your decision for you, but if it was me—"

He had a point.

"Okay," I said, as we moved into the hallway. "The bathroom stays as is. What else?"

Total removal of the walls between bedroom, living room and dining room was a possibility, he said, provided we left every other support post in place.

"If you had a second floor, I wouldn't recommend it. But since it's only a crawl space and no one's going to be walking around up there—"

"Agreed."

"But where will you put all these—" He nodded toward the giant nudes of prowling Vince. "—if you've got no walls to hang them on?"

"I'll still have my outer walls, won't I?"

"Well, sure—but they've got windows."

"I don't mind covering them."

Nate looked at me quizzically for a moment, before brightening.

"Then, hey, no problem!" he laughed.

"I'm concerned about the support posts, though."

"How so?"

"They seem so dull in their raw state."

"What do you want to do about them?"

The way he asked this, I thought he might be about to offer a suggestion. When none came, I said: "Maybe elaborate on them a little?"

"What do you mean: 'elaborate'?"

I led him toward the living-room coffee table.

"Here," I said. "Take a look at this."

I handed him a book about the ruins at Khajuraho: the erotic sculptures nestled in the alcoves of the temple walls. He leafed through it, pausing at some pages to cast a glance up at Vince, as if to confirm the accuracy of certain anatomical details.

"Ever been to India?" I asked.

"Nope, never," he said, blushing, eyes back on the book.

"Me neither," I told him, hoping to make him feel more comfortable.

After absorbing the rest of the book's contents as briskly as he could, he handed it back and said, "Problem is—you don't have much to work with."

"What do you mean?"

"Even the biggest posts are only four-by-six. That doesn't leave much leeway for carving."

"So what do you suggest?"

"Give me a week or two. I'll get back to you."

"Okay."

Then, as if to seal a deal I hadn't quite known we were making, he leaned in close and said, sotto voce: "Seriously, man—I'd *love* to come in on this with you."

VII. STAGE-PROP UNIVERSE

A little obliteration makes the world go round. The shell needs to break before the creature can emerge.

Violetta, when she finally got around to inspecting my progress, raised the bar well beyond what the other three—even her more-than-willing husband—had managed.

In her luscious, tobacco-cured Peruvian lilt, she murmured, "Ah, *amigo*—it's taking you a little longer than expected, no?"

She touched my shoulder consolingly, then slid her hand down my chest. Her sharply-nailed forefinger grazed my left nipple through my T-shirt, before she whisked it away and turned to look at Nate's handiwork. His carvings might not be up to Khajuraho standards. But he had captured the spirit I was after.

The four-by-six support posts were adorned with vertical walnut panels embossed with slender, twining figures exploring every sexual possibility imaginable, as well as some pretzel-like configurations that weren't decipherably sexual at all. You could sense the shy and husky Nate in each of them, even as you realized he would never act out any of these fantasies in the flesh. Instead, he was an earnest acolyte ardently striving—as dedicated to these shrines he'd created as he was unworthy of them. You could see how far this carnal calligraphy had lured him from his comfort zone, and yet how short of the mark it fell for him.

Violetta, caressing his bas reliefs, moved from one support post to another.

"In Iquitos, we had something like this," she said.

"Did you?"

"Only it was made of stone, not timber."

As she circulated through Nate's handiwork, a thoughtful look appeared on her face.

"When did he get all this done?" she asked. "He told me he was booked up through August. We wanted him for our new kitchen counter."

"He's been at it every weeknight and weekend."

"Well, he made a tidy job of it."

She was right. Nate was a professional. The living room, dining room and bedroom were immaculate. Every last trace of plaster and particle board had been removed from them. The hardwood floors had been scrubbed and polished to the point where his bas-relief orgies were softly reflected in a hickory sheen below. Cocks slid in from in front or behind, quite oblivious to questions of gender-pairing. Vi considered this, then shrugged it off to look again at my enlargements of her husband, spinning his own gelatin-silver variations on the priapism of the house posts. Interspersed with him now were photographs I'd taken of Nate and Mel in equally revealing postures.

My neighbors to the north, despite the sensual nature of Nate's carvings, had shied away from an overtly sexual approach. I found them both attractive, but they had trouble seeing themselves that way. They preferred blood sacrifice.

The photograph of Nate was particularly energizing. His grin was pained and ecstatic. The great thing about it was that it had happened so naturally—a mere slip of his hand against the skill saw, followed by a guttural "Oh fuck."

We just had time to shoot the photo and wrap his finger in ice, before heading to the Emergency Room where his severed digit, dangling by a fold of finger-skin, was reattached with surprisingly little damage to show for it.

Melanie, not to be outdone, had come up with her own special brand of martyrdom.

Bringing me casseroles, brownies and sample shampoos, she talked at length about the "chemical miracle" of human hair.

"It's almost enough to make you believe in God," she said, "or at least in some kind of hair god. Or jeez—!" she laughed. "Maybe I've just worked at that place too long."

"No, no," I urged her. "Keep going. This could be useful."

I had known that hair-care was her job. I hadn't known it was her passion.

"Well, the main ingredient is keratin," she continued. "It's a protein formed from eighteen amino acids, and it's organized in the cortex almost like an engineer did it to make a rope or cable. I mean, it's really strong! If you tied a cinder block to it and let it drop, it's your scalp that would give way, not the hair itself."

As she enthused about lipids, melatonin and sebaceous glands, her walk slowed, her gaze wandered and her monologue gradually faltered. She looked at the elaborate carvings her husband had made, at my enormous image of him with a bleeding stump for a finger, and at the now perfectly passable gaps between living room, dining room and bedroom. And then, as though these openings posed impossible impediments for her, she came to a complete halt and stammered: "I just don't—I really don't—see how you and Nate had time to *do* all this!"

From the forlorn way she said it, I could sense that she felt overlooked by us in some crucial and inconsiderate manner.

I had to mask my impatience with her ("Ask me *why*, goddamit!") and declared that I wasn't in any particular rush: "I plan on taking all the time that's needed."

At this, she succumbed to a mood more restless than any I had seen in her before—followed by a change of expression that made obvious her sudden urge to take action.

She couldn't have startled me more with what she came up with the next day. It was a sacrifice of a different kind entirely— as Violetta, continuing her house tour a week or so later, couldn't help but notice. And it quite held its own next to prowling Vince and bleeding Nate.

"*Dios mío!*" Vi exclaimed. "When did *this* happen?"

"Just this week."

She looked at the evidence more closely.

In the huge silver-gelatin print I'd made of Melanie, she

stared out with a mixture of horror at what she had done and triumph that she'd been able to do it. From the contrast between the panic in her eyes and the determination of her pose, you could feel the sickly sinking sensations that had overcome her as I snapped the shutter.

She had shaved her head so closely it seemed no hair had ever grown there. Her scalp glistened as if floor wax had been used to polish it. In her hand she gripped her shorn-off golden locks. They resembled a small strangled animal.

The tension in the photograph was almost unbearable—felicitously so.

My props were all in place, now, arrayed around the rooms. But "rooms"—as Violetta demonstrated as she slipped from one wall-less space to another—was something of a misnomer. How could you call them "rooms" when there were no obstructions left between them?

Still, Vi surprised me when she said, "You could take this further, you know."

"You think?"

"No matter how far you go," she purred, "there's always another step to take."

VIII. DEADLY REVISER

People passing in the street would look my way and joke, "Camping out, huh?"

They had it half-right. Doing without walls was a bit like living in a tent—if you mean a tent made solely of tent poles, without any confining canvas....

Sledgehammers and vacuum cleaners hadn't been adequate to the task. Axes, chainsaws and wood shredders were more the ticket.

Naturally, this made quite a racket—a racket that got the attention of my neighbors.

From the north, Nate came charging out the minute he saw me swinging my axe at my outer walls. For such a heavy-set fellow he could move quite quickly—but it left him panting.

"Dude!—ah—dude!" he said between gasps for breath. "You want to watch what you're doing there. You could bring the whole place down!"

This was, perhaps, what I had expected—but it wasn't what I wanted to hear.

To drown it out, I turned on the chainsaw. Nate made as if to grab it from me. But catching the warning look in my eye, he held back.

From the south Violetta emerged in a colorful mini-dress and black spiked heels. Her long black hair, I saw, was tied in a top knot secured by a rainbow-colored scarf. She was petite but wiry, and surprisingly strong.

And she was ready to get down to business.

The chop of her axe as it slammed into her house must be ringing out as resonantly as mine had, but it was impossible to hear it over the chainsaw. Nate, in the meantime, hardly knew which way to turn. He stepped toward Vi, then scurried back to me, apparently viewing my situation with more urgency.

After a minute or two, wearying of him jumping up and down, shouting inaudible alarms, I turned the chainsaw off to let him have his say. Nearby bird-song and far-off highway noise echoed around us, punctuated by the "crunches" of Violetta's axe, every bit as delicious as I'd thought they might be.

"Yes," I said. "What is it?"

"Seriously, dude, that's your last structural support post there. If you get rid of it, that whole corner might come down."

"Well, we'll see, shall we?"

"See?"

"See what it's like without it."

Nate, stumped for the moment, just stared at me. And then, with the light going out of his eyes, he retreated to his house—perhaps to formulate some new argument.

Whatever he came up with, I was sure, would be to no avail. The house, it seemed to me lately, had become a crutch to my existence—a crutch that I could do without. Still, I had some pity for him. And it's funny how having a dab of pity for someone can make you relent somewhat.

Setting the chainsaw aside, I retrieved my axe and walked around to Vince and Vi's side of my house, out of Nate's sight. There, I engaged in a steady rhythmic counterpoint to Violetta's firm blows.

This was hot work, and as the siding splintered in the warm summer breeze, I began to strip down. I also got a better view of the progress Vi was making and the sights she was disclosing as the interior of her and Vincent's house came into view.

Clad only in a black nylon sports brassiere and Lycra briefs now, she looked marvelous. The way she pivoted on her spiked heels brought to mind some Olympic event in which sturdy women showed the centrifugal ways they could hurl a shot-put or a discus. She was all aglow.

Inside the house, Vince was aglow too. If he'd ever had a job, he must have abandoned it. He hadn't left home for weeks. His sole purpose in life these days seemed to be to wander in a bobbing tumescent state through rooms that had once been separate from one another. His exhibitionism had more to do with an expansion of horizons than an urge toward sex. And yet it was quite stimulating in its own right.

I was aroused, at any rate—and in this state, ten minutes later, I walked back over toward Nate and Mel's house to catch up with developments on that front.

Their home was still intact. But activities within had taken a turn I wasn't expecting.

It's sad, I think, when friends who want to compete can't agree on their terms of competition. Nate and Mel were all too aware of the progress that Vincent, Violetta and I were making, and they wanted to be a part of it.

The "why," of course, eluded them completely, and they seemed to be aware of this. To compensate, they'd made some character-shattering initiatives of their own—actions that seemed both to the purpose and utterly at odds with the things that were trying to happen.

In an upstairs window, a shirtless Nate, looming large, looked to his right and to his left, before withdrawing into the shadows. It was as though he wanted to mimic Vincent without exposing himself completely. Meanwhile on the ground floor in their dining-room bay window, Mel had inflicted herself with cuts and scars that sat uneasily on her bald shampoo-girl features. On her face a desperate question was written which, if you had to put it into words, might be: "Is this what you wanted? Am I getting it right?"

My silent response, which she interpreted all too accurately, left her in a turbulent state.

In the meantime, Vince and Vi carried on as sexily and serenely as ever. Sports bra now discarded, Vi resembled some topless female warrior of ancient legend. Her sylph-like figure was well-suited to its mission of destruction. But even she had her limits when it came to stamina.

Taking a break, she strolled over to my place and, nodding toward Nate and Mel, asked: "What's up with them?"

I turned to take fresh note of their antics.

Nate was shimmying in his window like an overweight burlesque dancer. Mel, with a safety pin, was trying to pierce things—a cheek, a lip, a nostril—that she'd never pierced before

"I'm not sure," I said, "but it's been going on for a while now."

Vi gave them a friendly wave, which they answered with pained smiles and tentative waves back at her. Then she headed off, axe in hand. Time was growing short, and she still had a lot of house left to deal with.

Nate, after she'd gone, hurried over to me, eager to hear what she'd had to say and how he might act on it. He was particularly anxious to know how much longer this "contest," as he called it, would last.

"I mean, how far do you think they're ahead of us?"

I looked at his and Mel's place, and then toward Vince and Vi's, before shaking my head.

"I'm sorry. If you have to ask...."

He looked down at the sidewalk, shame-faced, disappointed.

I turned away from him. Worried that Vi might be pulling ahead of me, I took a hefty sledgehammer-swing at my open dining room's last remaining corner support.

At precisely the moment when I hit my mark, Nate, unable to help himself, sprang toward me, hairy breasts bouncing, trying to foil my actions.

Too late. The whole business—ceiling, gutters, shingled roof—began to groan and slide down, exactly as he had predicted.

It caught him at an angle on the temple, knocking him out and burying him in choking debris.

IX. VIVA NOWHERE

I increasingly had the feeling that if someone had asked me "why" I was doing the things I was doing (an "if" that seemed less and less likely), all I'd be able to say would be: "I haven't got a clue—but if you'd care to join me...."

No walls, no floors, no windows, no ceilings. The only thing left was a giant pile of abandoned pick-up sticks. Even the photographs of Mel, Nate and Vince were crumpled under the mess, inaccessible.

Vince and Vi, acknowledging I was the victor, had slowed things down a bit and were giving themselves more time to savor each stage of their demolition.

We were all of us naked now, except for Mel who insisted on maintaining a rudimentary sense of costume even as she disfigured herself in every other way.

No such problem with Nate. I'd been able to lend him a hand in death as I could never have managed it in life. His crushed head and torso were pinned under my dining-room ceiling and rafters. But his sneakers and trousers and underwear were easy enough to remove, the wreckage holding him in place as I tugged them off him.

It was touching to see that, as hard as he had fought against us, cautioning us about the dangers we were courting, he nevertheless had been excited enough about our agenda to sport a semi-erect response to it, even in demise. Too shy to share this arousal with us while living, he now offered the vestiges of it for all to see.

Vincent and Violetta, joining me, took note of Nate's "afterglow" and gathered strength from it, too—enough, eventually, to create a fully dismantled Eden for themselves. The entire neighborhood, in fact, was ringing now with the sound of axes and sledge-hammers and gas-powered implements of destruction. Smoking fires rose from burning kitchens, increasing our carbon footprint by leaps and bounds.

When would we be done with this? How soon would we be able to let it go?

We were waiting for some "tomorrow," it felt like—a day that kept receding as we approached it, and perhaps never would come....

X. INSIDE THE BUFFER ZONE

Gone is gone. Razed is razed. Demolished is demolished.

We squatted to do our business in the ruins. We fucked whoever happened to need fucking. We drank out of such fetid pools as were available to us.

True, there were holdouts—folks who simply wouldn't get with the program. And Mel, in her dining-room window, was an intractable case if ever there was one.

She was a mess of overlapping cranial scars. She was a welter of bleeding tattoos and fresh facial mutilations. But in terms of home-upkeep and wardrobe, she remained impeccable. She vacuumed daily, scrubbed every surface that needed scrubbing and even touched up Nate's original paint-jobs, both inside the house and outside it. She had taken her place, determinedly, in a sort of buffer zone, waiting for the destruction she could see playing out on every side of her to overwhelm her. But she wasn't going to give it an inch of her own volition. And by placing herself inside this buffer zone, she had trapped us in it too. We couldn't complete our trajectories until she deigned to join us—and that didn't seem likely to happen any time soon.

The only concession she granted was to undo her blouse a button or two at a time, revealing a little cleavage before buttoning it right back up. Or she might, as a rare treat, "accidentally" spill some dirt from her dustpan onto her front steps, letting it sit there for only a moment before she swept it up and deposited it in her garbage can.

I had to admire her strength of purpose, however perverse it seemed to me. If I were to approach her—if I were to walk toward the only house left standing for blocks around—would she look at me, in all my unclothed glory, and look at her husband, in all of his, and change course at last? Would she finally consent to take part in our endeavor and let the things happen that were trying to happen? Or would she simply keep hacking at her face and distorting her features, consulting her compact-mirror as she did so?

The way she dug in, the way she persisted, was a sight to see—even if it made life a limbo for the rest of us.

I was the lens through which to view these events. Vi was an Amazonian abstraction, tensile in her strength. Vince was a dream she'd had, his prick a gift for all the world to savor. Nate was rich flesh under the downed structure of my house—and I had no clue how to extract him.

As for Melanie, she was triumphant.

It takes only one bad egg to spoil the whole nest, it seems.

The longer she held on, the more she put obstacles in our paths. And the tidier she kept herself, the further she thwarted all the things that were trying—still trying!—at every conceivable level and on every possible front to happen.

from *When Two Are In Love or As I Came To Behind Frank's Transporter*

Philip Terry & James Davies

31

The waiter, who'd grown fond of us, brought out some raspy herb liquor as a digestif. It was hard to stomach but we liked him; he let us smoke our cigarettes inside.

The waiter, who'd grown fond of us, brought out some raspy herb liquor as a digestif. It was hard to stomach but we liked him; he let us smoke our **Camels** inside.

The waiter, who'd grown fond of us, brought out some raspy herb liquor as a digestif. It was hard to stomach but we liked him; he let us smoke **twenty Camels** inside.

The **shaman**, who'd grown fond of us, brought out some raspy herb liquor as a digestif. It was hard to stomach but we liked him; he let us smoke **twenty Camels** inside.

The **shaman**, who'd grown fond of us, brought out some raspy herb liquor as a **motif**. It was hard to stomach but we liked him; he let us smoke **twenty Camels** inside.

The **shaman**, who'd grown fond **for** us, brought out some raspy herb liquor as a **motif**. It was hard to stomach but we liked him; he let us smoke **twenty Camels** inside.

The **shaman**, who'd grown fond **for** us, brought out some raspy herb **vicars** as a **motif**. It was hard to stomach but we liked him; he let us smoke **twenty Camels** inside.

The **shaman**, who'd grown **marijuana for** us, brought out some raspy herb **vicars** as a **motif**. It was hard to stomach but we liked him; he let us smoke **twenty Camels** inside.

The **shaman**, who'd grown **marijuana for** us, brought out **nineteen** raspy herb **vicars** as a **motif**. It was hard to stomach but we liked him; he let us smoke **twenty Camels** inside.

The **shaman**, who'd grown **marijuana for** us, brought out **nineteen** raspy **TV vicars** as a **motif**. It was hard to stomach but we liked him; he let us smoke **twenty Camels** inside.

The **shaman**, who'd grown **marijuana for** us, brought out **nineteen hundred TV vicars** as a **motif**. It was hard to stomach but we liked him; he let us smoke **twenty Camels** inside.

The **shaman**, who'd grown **marijuana for** us, brought out **nineteen hundred TV vicars** as a **motif**. It was hard to stomach but we liked him; he let us **exercise twenty camels** inside.

The **shaman**, who'd grown **marijuana for** us, brought out **nineteen hundred TV vicars** as **leitmotif**. It was hard to stomach but we liked him; he let us **exercise twenty camels** inside.

The **shaman**, who'd grown **marijuana for Petra**, brought out **nineteen hundred TV vicars** as **leitmotif**. It was hard to stomach but we liked him; he let us **exercise twenty camels** inside.

The **shaman,** who'd grown **marijuana for Petra,** brought out **nineteen hundred TV vicars** as **leitmotif**. It was hard to **process** but we liked him; he let us **exercise twenty camels** inside.

The **shaman,** who'd grown **marijuana for Petra,** brought out **nineteen hundred TV vicars** as **leitmotif**. It was hard to **process** but we **humoured** him; he let us **exercise twenty camels** inside.

The **shaman,** who'd grown **marijuana for Petra,** brought out **nineteen hundred TV vicars** as **leitmotif**. It was hard to **process** but we **humoured** him; he **made us exercise twenty camels** inside.

The **shaman,** who'd grown **marijuana for Petra,** brought out **nineteen hundred TV vicars** as **leitmotif**. It was hard to **process** but we **humoured** him; he **made Wolf exercise twenty camels** inside.

Chris Shaman, who'd grown **marijuana for Petra,** brought out **nineteen hundred TV vicars** as **leitmotif**. It was hard to **process** but we **humoured** him; he **made Wolf exercise twenty camels** inside.

Chris Shaman, who'd grown **marijuana for Petra,** brought **down nineteen hundred TV vicars** as **leitmotif**. It was hard to **process** but we **humoured** him; he **made Wolf exercise twenty camels** inside.

Chris Shaman, who'd grown **marijuana for Petra,** brought **down nineteen hundred TV vicars** as **leitmotif**. It was hard to **process** but we **humoured** him; **Chris made Wolf exercise twenty camels** inside.

Chris Shaman, who'd grown **marijuana for Petra, noted down 1900s TV vicars** as **leitmotif**. It was hard to **process** but we **humoured** him; **Chris made Wolf exercise twenty camels** inside.

Chris Shaman, who'd grown **marijuana for Petra, noted down 1900s TV vicars** as **leitmotif**. It was hard to **process** but we **humoured her;Chris made Wolf exercise twenty camels** inside.

Chris Shaman, who'd grown **marijuana for Petra, noted down 1900s TV vicars** as **leitmotif**. It was hard to **process** but we **humoured her; Chris made Wolf exercise twenty camels back-to-back.**

Chris Shaman, who'd grown **marijuana for Petra, noted down 1900s TV vicars** as **leitmotif**. It was hard **this process** but we **humoured her; Chris made Wolf exercise twenty camels back-to-back.**

Chris Shaman, who'd grown **marijuana for Petra, noted down 1900s TV vicars (her leitmotif).** It was hard **this process** but we **humoured her; Chris made Wolf exercise twenty camels back-to-back.**

Chris Shaman, **(she'd** grown **marijuana for Petra) noted down 1900s TV vicars (her leitmotif).** It was hard **this process** but we **humoured her; Chris made Wolf exercise twenty camels back-to-back.**

Chris Shaman, **(she'd smuggled marijuana for Petra) noted down 1900s TV vicars (her leitmotif).** It was hard **this process** but we **humoured her; Chris made Wolf exercise twenty camels back-to-back.**

Chris Shaman, **(she'd smuggled marijuana for Petra) noted down 1900s TV vicars (her leitmotif).** It was hard **this process** but **Petra humoured her; Chris made Wolf exercise twenty camels back-to-back.**

Chris Shaman, **(she'd smuggled marijuana for Petra) noted down 1900s TV vicars (her leitmotif).** It **wasn't** hard **this process** but **Petra humoured her; Chris made Wolf exercise twenty camels back-to-back.**

Chris Shaman, **(she'd smuggled marijuana for Petra) noted down 1900s TV vicars (her leitmotif). This wasn't** hard **this process** but **Petra humoured her; Chris made Wolf exercise twenty camels back-to-back.**

Chris Shaman, (she'd smuggled marijuana for Petra) noted down 1900s TV vicars (her leitmotif). This wasn't unobsessional this process but Petra humoured her; Chris made Wolf exercise twenty camels back-to-back.

Chris Shaman, (she'd smuggled marijuana for Petra) noted down 1900s TV vicars (her leitmotif). This wasn't unobsessional this process yet Petra humoured her. Chris made Wolf exercise twenty Camels back-to-back.

from *Under the Gas Museum*

a collaborative invention in three parts

John Hall & Peter Hughes

Part 1: Chapter 1

In which:

i.   is considered a notion of moveable parts and their relation both to possible wholes and to possession

ii.   one of our narrators claims prior right to gaze outwards

iii.   the museum is not the Gas Museum

iv.   it is instead, possibly, the Museum of Restored Wholes

v.   the silent sounds of being wrong grow loud, we hear the names of Simon and Elizabeth (Beth?) and may be stuck in a loop with musicians who are near neighbours in the alphabet

vi.   we regret Simon and Elizabeth's pasts in poor novels and consider the demerits of taxonomy

vii.   Antonio finds himself outside on the gravel

viii.   Cannonball Adderley and Jack Kerouac are both long dead and Antonio's tendency to 'find himself' is considered

ix.   Liqiu and Antonio's key are stuck in traffic and Art Pepper's 'What is this thing ... ?' fails to reach the end of the question

x.   Antonio's solution, despite his precarious situation, is to do nothing

'Mine!' in competitive shouts of up over the playground. Working from parts to whole in acts of construction which presuppose prior labour, entrepreneurial feats of gainful analysis with predictive synthetic outcomes. First Meccano then Lego. And what of the acts of interpretation when parts aren't already conveniently sorted? Mine! The same parts suggesting different wholes that have to be inferred. This gestalt is mine. Whose what? And have you been paid? All these 'mines' parts of speech. Why presume that they are all the same parts or that the verbs carry the same moods? And what is this whole that they are part of? Each child's 'mine!' lifting above the playground, some more stridently than others. A whole a matter of tone and mood.

This one isn't mine it's yours. You'd think by now we'd be able to avoid these confusions. It's not as if we haven't had experiences, or thoughts. Some of that experience we had at the same time in the same place but after that it's all norture. Different environments prepare different effects, even the view from your bedroom window, which was mine. We start to plan constructions and can't agree on building blocks. This time I'm resorting to compressed bread. Do you remember when the car swept into the driveway that night and painted the hallway with fear? I still can't make sense of all her scattered notes. How is Liqiu by the way? I have these crossword answers in my wallet and I was wondering if you could provide the questions again. Torrent. Isotope. Pecorino.

You must parse your prose into its parts. I can't cope with so many anxieties all jostling for my limited attention. And, please, no claims on that view. I have built a career on it, gazing so many years from that window and relaying my meditations through the usual outlets. Gazing outwards provides protection or displacement from the troublingly haunted hallway, the only other way out for the mind. I think that this was Liqiu's undoing. She is suffering now from a kind of aphasia in which on different days different parts of speech are impaired. Yesterday the confusion over prepositions was particularly troubling: she got stuck on 'behind' and was alarmed when I took her literally. However, you could try her on your cross-word puzzle questions, especially a highly conceptual noun like isotope. Pecorino will be more of a problem.

It turned out to be a whole cupful of freshly-ground black pepper. Yet neither the person staring through the window nor the view would ever stay the same for long enough to sketch out the extension. It's one thing to make a model on the kitchen table, quite another to bring it to fruition in the county. A section of my coding packed up in 1965 and has only recently been opened up as a museum. It has a certain dusty lustre but everyone knows it's basically a work-experience spokesperson in the wrong venue on the last day of October. We forgot that we'd stored anything of any interest or value in the attic of the old house before we moved to the 1980s flat. We remembered three days after the old house burned down. The whole is always falling off the table.

Well, we are both as one on this at least: that views and wholes are unstable, despite everything. Despite in particular that those who gaze from windows do so in expectation of a sense of wholeness that visual control of distance can offer them. And auditory control too, of course. Those cries from the playground are not competing with me, and that, after all, is the point. Quietly observe and listen with your back to all the troubles. Except that I heard the cries as I swept past in the car and, as you know, drivers must attend to the closer-to-hand, whatever their passengers are taking in. And as for you, did you think that grinding far more pepper than one dish could ever call for somehow makes you ready for everything, even reassembling all those wholes that have fallen off the table, nearly out of memory. I am glad you have discovered the Museum of Restored Wholes, though. (I assume that's what you are referring to?) Perhaps we could meet there? If we do, could you reassure me that the meeting will be amicable? After all, I will have had to make my way out through that hallway, which is liable to stir up again all the bad feelings.

Aren't you forgetting the recipients of the grant? Or was it just a rebate? Simon and Elizabeth had both appeared in mediocre novels during that first destructive decade of the century. But it had led to nothing. Moving into Widow's Peak, like every other decision, had been an exaggerated and inappropriate reaction to misunderstood events over the preceding months. As soon as the last dark cardigan had been unpacked and hung in the dilapidated wardrobe, the silent sounds of being wrong grew loud. The wardrobe leaned away from the damp wall, its seams gaping, a self-assembly fiasco from years ago, too perfect a metaphor to be included in any rigorous inventory. More significantly, all the previous episodes took on the characteristics of children's building blocks from incompatible sets. In each case the sizes didn't match, the studs wouldn't fit, and the materials had a different density and sheen each from the other. There was even a sense that the kits were out on loan and could be recalled at any moment. And who can embark on a meaningful project under those conditions? The sky didn't even go with the ground. Neither Liqiu nor Antonio felt in control of a narrative. The suitors all expected a novel in the spirit of Calvino. Beth tinkered with the text throughout the afternoons but later, while the suitors watched slovenly tales of urban matchmaking on Netflix, she transformed each page of prose into minimalist poems made from one cupful of syllables each. Before test driving the hologram of completion, we need to rope in the extras. And with so many rules already imposed from the outside why do we make up so many more to impose upon ourselves? For more months than 'I care to remember' I've been unable to listen to the music of anyone whose surname doesn't begin with B. I hoped to be moving on to Sir Granville Bantock by the beginning of November but it already seems too late.

I supposed at first that I should thank you for reminding me of the grant but then I read on through your dismal recital of everything that had gone rather tediously wrong and how much of this was associated with the grant, including those two – Simon and Elizabeth, I mean – who seem really to have believed that they could escape their separate and joint inadequacies by hiding in second rate novels, exactly the kinds of stories in my experience that aim from the first page at restoring finally the very lack of wholeness that they relentlessly disrupt. You know, don't you, that there is a room in the Museum where you can see three or four such novels laid out in their supposed 'parts' and that the shop sells these in kit-form with instructions not unlike those for assembling failing wardrobes? It never works because you never know whether or not the joints should show. And this kind of whole is just beyond any such experience, however much Simon and Elizabeth bleat about it, and that's the point. When you have been through Basie and Braxton your eye moves along the damp shelf to Coleman, Coltrane and Davis. But we may be looking at different shelves. There never was a taxonomy that wasn't born out of a will for coherence. (And every taxonomy assumes at least a single if not a a double negation?)

I have made an exception for Cannonball Adderley – those master tapes from the Riverside days. The kits don't work, especially those they cynically market as 'kites'. But what advice is there to give to oneself? Antonio found himself outside on the gravel, staring through the window of his own flat. A TV drama was never about to unfold. Sometimes when you stop moving it feels as though death is catching up with you, probably through those woods over to the west; or maybe through fumes from the foundations. You whistle old songs about rivers. You hum creaky tracks about roads which no longer exist. For a few seconds you even consider re-reading Kerouac. But there's always so much more to be said about even the most minor character before the story can be started with any conviction – the switch thrown, the carousel set spinning. It's better with your eyes closed. It's better with your eyes closed and your headphones on. My progress has also been hampered by the discovery of thirteen more composers called Bach. The old nightmares have come back as well. I'm in a sensory-deprivation tank and all my senses are working perfectly. But the water has lost some of its warmth.

I sense here a grasping for simplifying solutions, not so much a struggle to apprehend wholes as an exclusive selection of privileged parts, some of them purely magical. B indeed! I also sense a set of tactics for making do with the nearly intolerable. Though I do like your calling again of the name of Kerouac. Didn't he try to defy the divisive effect of parts called pages with that famous roll?

But perhaps we could take Antonio as a case study. Antonio has always, ever since I have known him, had a tendency to 'find himself' somewhere as though the story that got him to that position could be annulled, just not told, even to himself. I envy that. It would lighten the burden of responsibility for one's own actions. Why not assign them entirely to another author? I 'find myself' picturing Antonio, staring up at his window, out of which no one gazes, with the faint sound of Cannonball repeating a phrase over and over again because the stylus is stuck and there is no way of lifting the arm off the record from down there on the gravel. He listens to the sound of a sonic part mesmerizingly failing to connect or end and contrasts it with the image in his head of the subtle and intricate interconnection of parts that make up the stylus arm. Could you say that Adderley 'finds himself' caught in repetition or is it now nothing to do with him? He and Kerouac are both long dead. It is Antonio who finds himself thus and now we do too, stuck with trying to imagine what the phrase is that is doomed to repetition until Antonio can find his way back in, through that hallway, and up the stairs. How easy it is in his head to lift that arm. How many times he does so.

The pressure of attention, it has to come in waves. Is concentration rhythmic? Can reading a painting help as a model? Relentlessness becomes mechanical. No-one wants to tap-dance in the stocks. What about dance suites? Try one of these biscuits. At the end of any section there's an opportunity for the mind to ripple over leagues of probability. This creates a useful setting for that which happens next. Liqiu was a little behind and the only one with a spare key to Antonio's place. She sat in traffic, Art Pepper tripping through the speakers. So many versions of the stuck phrase, the first six notes of 'What is this thing called love?' Difficult to imagine a more annoying phrase to stick – especially as it was only half a phrase really. The sixth note stands on the end of a plank peering through the mist in search of the twelfth. But it's looking the wrong way. Antonio had once made the mistake of including a real author as a character in one of his botched novellas. But if you're going to rope in Erri de Luca as a member of your cast, you need to think hard about what words to put into his mouth. Especially when they are recounting part of your own crippled story. It had probably needed more magic, not less. At any rate, Antonio was not aspiring to any kind of solution. He just wanted to make it to the end of the day. So many phrases were stuck on interior loops. The alternative, if some tiny motion upwards could be effected, was silence.

Making it to the end of the day is, after all, some kind of solution, repeated every day until finally not. Unless, that is, you've wandered into the wrong kind of novel, the kind where forced entry alone is ground for slaughter. Antonio contemplated the drain pipe, trying to assess if, with the window open as it was, he could shimmy up and then risk a leap to his left with his left hand ready to grasp at the window edge. Risky perhaps but that repeated unfinished phrase was getting troublesome. He probably would have tried, risking a fall on to the gravel, but other thoughts that he had been entertaining simultaneously slowed down the impulse much as that stuck record would slow if it were being played on a wind-up. Mostly two other thoughts, but who can decide on borders in such cases? What dialogue should he give Erri de Luca? Should he plunder something from that author's own work, perhaps putting it through some form of transformation that concealed the theft but retained the rhythms? Should he also risk involving Liqiu, so that she could at least behave and speak in a way over which he had some control. He wondered if that was in the end what his writing was for and if that was why he so often got himself stuck on a phrase. Liqiu was the second thought, already entwined, as you can see, in the first. She had his key and was late. His relief on her eventual arrival was likely to make him angry with her. That was not a good idea. How could he be stuck with weighing up so many different risks all at once? The solution, if that's what it was, was to do nothing.

from *Ignore Previous*,

collaborative inventions in 11 cantos

John Hall & Peter Hughes

Canto 1

1

I dreamed about the zenlessness of scaffolding
a universe full of light & airy cages
each one invisible

> my life was in a very dark patch for ages
> nothing I tried seemed to be working for me
> and then light and air came

2

and when I came to I could see the dark framework
that held this cavernous universe in space
and I was scared for ages

> flooding through the tears in my worn material
> waking up my senses with a few new voices
> a mesh of fresh foundations

3

I'd been channeling stuffed polar bears in Leicester
& knocking out cold & still-born pages saying
'Please do not touch Peppy'

> transforming not removing the rare sense of fear
> now stirring me to find the light of redemption
> in the second half of my life

4

and now I knew that this would no longer do for me
trapped between seeing the cage and seeing the void
both reprehensible

> reading the triumph of life again didn't help
> & a holiday with Dante renewed my fears
> of theological cages

5

so I found myself resorting to the local
manifestations of nature & resistance
humanity & star-gazing

> I said to myself that there is no redemption
> in ideas alone whose abstract lonely distance
> craves the sensuous life of things

6

and a similar problem occurred though this time
cosmic in its elevation with night void
and scaffolding of stars

> warm south-westerlies redolent of mackerel
> & thyme spoke of that which brings me to my knees
> every day in the garden

7

the central consolation being the extent
to which the void made this small green fist of life
more strangely beautiful

      attending to seedlings as though to the newest life
      sensuous in their green vulnerability
      while grievous fish are in the air

8

but consolation is of its nature never
enough even with the rewards of strange beauty
when the void remains

      & where the void became ideas to release
      & daily flush away into the zenlessness
      of our transient atmosphere

9

avoiding definition of the void becomes
the one preoccupation of the mind
joined to the other

      then I knew that this could no longer be the void
      since in the void there can be no ideas at all
      least of all of lessnessness

10

and hear me here avoid a void or at least urge
myself and others to do so aiming thereby
to end abandonment of hope

      is it the mind's work to pop brackets round (the void)
      in order to continue serving the sentence
      ordained by time

11

the scaffold needs a ladder made of two long sticks
which don't usually meet but are connected
by several short sticks or steps

>   the paradoxical racket of the silence
>   of the old sound-vacuum we think of as the (void)
>   rickety discord of the spheres

Canto 2

1

Here's the circus with Italian panda-dogs
(they're certainly worth googling)
distracting us from the all-engulfing wasteland

>   not a dip or rise in sight the plain flattens out
>   tranquillity of remembrance
>   its spatial expanse obliterating lines of time

2

and at the same time causing us to speculate
on the mysterious arrival
without wake of dust to betray its recent past

>   the ghostly assemblies of most of a lifetime
>   shimmer in midsummer dusk
>   faint blue July lines are converging behind us

3

a savage reformation of the atmosphere
accompanies the earthly abuses
& millions stand in the swaying light of the fires

>   there is as yet no guide no sign of redemption
>   through a right choice of path
>   but only this venal gloom darkened by corruption

4

having only a dim sense that their own actions
had added to this savagery
mostly through variations of greed and vanity

      the prissy orchestration of paranoia
      scrambles all sense of direction
      but it seems the road out of here now heads downwards

5

I calmly sing of devastating rhetoric
deployed by the corporate press
to fine tune prejudice & fear savagely

      so it is now downwards we are condemned to go
      not knowing why or who leads us
      who knows it may be some obscure knowledge we crave

6

a savage rhetoric just like paranoia
has its undertow of truth
angry contempt is the miasma of these plains

      as it all goes downhill we keep it company
      & examine the foundations
      of our remaining groundedness & of our vision

7

maybe that river or mirage in the distance
will freshen our perspectives
perhaps we'll reach its banks before darkness falls

      these foundations are it must be said unsettling
      the solid earth above
      is no more solid than the honeycomb of cells

8

or perhaps we will do no more than reach the point
where we can discern
if it is the river known to induce mirages

so much of the earth is made of ruin compressed
into a temporary growing medium
fenced off & funded for a few baleful harvests

9

the river is illuminated by late light
echoing songs of redemption
though what is carried where remains a mystery

a negative compost formed out of toxic waste
pressed by the feet of the lost
in their directionless pacing of the plain above

10

most music promises melancholy redemption
which is why the wise Odysseus
filled his ears with wax against the Sirens' promise

the geomorphology of the mind buckles
heights & depths are misaligned
igneous extrusions call out in foreign tongues

11

in the heart of the wasteland stands a single oar
site of a long-departed circus
a sign post which carries little information

unsure whether it is mind or the earth itself
whose hold on gravity
is fragile to the point of imminent fracture

Boarding School

Peter Quartermain

Brewood. Our Kid loves browsing around rag-and-bone shops looking for books, he's quite a dab hand at it, gets back home gleeful with his loot, especially if it's bound volumes of *Punch*, they're too heavy to read comfortably on your knee, at least they are for me, but he'll spend hours with one, listening with half an ear to a record or to music on the wireless in front of the fire in his worn saggy armchair, and he sounded quite chuffed, pleased with himself when he recited on the phone a really terrible limerick he came across in the February 16 1935 issue:

> An old-fashioned spinster from Brewood
> Was such an impossible prewood
> That she got in a state-o-
> Ver peeling potato
> And serving it up in the newood.

"Well," he said, after I said something about its attitude towards women, "yes. It *is* pretty awful. It's prissy, and it's lazy. That last line doesn't really rhyme, does it. But it's still a good way to tell strangers how to pronounce the village name." Of course all us kids took a certain pleasure in knowing that ordinary people wouldn't know how to spell it if they heard it, or how it *should* sound if they read it. Once

we got settled, *Brewood* was such an everyday word, how to say
it second nature, but like everybody else a tiny corner of me was
secretly proud of that knowing, it set us apart and said we belonged.
I could hardly believe my eyes when a few years later, at everyone's
insistence especially Marlow Grandfather's, I read a version of *Tom
Brown's Schooldays* which began with an epigraph cribbed from
the 1835 *Rugby School Magazine* saying that School is "a complete
social body, a society, in which by the nature of the case, we must
not only learn, but act and live; and act and live not only as boys,
but as boys who will be men." That idea, without me noticing it until I
read it, was drummed into me pretty much without pause, until I left
eleven years later.

Our Kid'd been there for over a year when I started at
Brewood. I was seven and a bit, and Mum came upstairs with
me and Phil to see the dormitory I'd be in. We met a grey-haired
woman in white, her clothes crackled and shooshed as she moved
about, she had a sitting room just round the corner where she
kept bandages and medicines and things as well as a warm fire
and a kettle, a table and comfy-looking chairs, when she breathed
there was this faint creaking her clothes were so stiff, and Mum
said "Matron will look after you, Peter, you'll be alright, won't he
Mrs Grant," Our Kid restlessly shifting his weight from one foot
to another, me holding onto Mum's hand, and Mrs Grant took my
other hand she smelled a bit like TCP antiseptic mixed with face
powder and Mum bent down and kissed me goodbye and turned
away to go downstairs, Our Kid already half-way down the hall on
his way to Dormitory Two to see his pals "Where did you go for the
summer?" "What did you do?" "Look at what I've got!" and I was
still watching after Mum when Matron took me into the dormitory to
meet the others, three of them watching another who was sitting on
a bed steering a toy car. It had a black cord stretching from a small
steering wheel sticking out of a box in his hand down to a shiny red
car on the floor and as he turned the wheel the car turned, I'd seen
one before, one of the kids I'd known in Shirley before the War had
had one, it said *Distler* underneath and a lot of funny words I couldn't
read, it looked just like a real sedan car, it wasn't a Dinky Toy much
too heavy, it had windows you could see through, with a couple of
batteries tucked away inside where you couldn't see them. "Too
expensive for us," Dad had said, "so's an electric train," we really

wanted one of those, a Hornby HO scale we'd seen pictures of on the back of *Meccano Magazine*, we knew someone who had one but not as fancy as in the pictures. "This is Gravette," said Matron, pointing to the boy with the car, "This is Quartermain Minor," she told us all each other's names, Smithe, Jones, Hart, "you're all in Prep class," and we stood around in silence, looking at each other when the other wasn't looking, shuffling our feet, gazing round the room, awkward faces. "Malpas is here too, he's in that bed" and she pointed to the bed under the window across from the door, "he's the senior boy in the dormitory, he was here last year. He'll show you round. And this," she said to me, "is your bed," with its tartan blanket, and a wooden locker at its head, "there's your trunk." I knew it was mine because it was brand new I'd been with Mum when she bought it along with the tartan at Beattie's in Wolverhampton, I could see where Dad had painted "P A Q" on the end the letters all shiny black under the handle. My bed was opposite the windows, and Hart followed my gaze and said "what's that tree? I've never seen anything like that" and I told him it was a monkey puzzle, proud to know something he didn't, but he didn't know whether to believe me or not, he was older than me, they all were. "There's only six of you here tonight," Matron said, "the others will be coming tomorrow, except for one," and I still recall trying to sleep that night, lying awake in that big half-empty room, the three empty beds, two patches of dim light stretched across the ceiling from the ventilators high in the white plank wall, one of them right over my bed, two glimmering huge truss beams their white bulk reaching across the room and through the ceiling, black iron stanchions a faint line sensed more than seen, one end of the beam disappearing out through the wall over my head and across the corridor outside, pressing down and reaching up in the same motion the space and shape opening up but pressing in, doubled shadows of beams stretching out and across and down the other side of the room in the gleam from the ventilators, a kind of roomy oppressiveness nothing at all like home, sounds of footsteps in the corridor outside, the HouseMaster or more likely the House Prefect patrolling, Malpas and Hart whispering to each other in the corner of the room, Gravette snuffling to himself, me missing Mum, wanting to be in my own bed with my battered yellow Teddy-bear, under my blue quilted eiderdown, the sound of the grandfather clock in the hall ticking away, Mum and Dad talking quietly. The room was so big, so cold and strange, no carpet on the floor not even a rug, echoes and noises from outside, the sheets so cold blankets so light, bedsprings creaking as somebody turned over, footsteps as someone in shoes climbed the cement stairs, the dim outlines of the two rows of beds, the chests of drawers at each end, an owl in the garden somewhere, the row of washbasins gleaming grey, the weight of my dressing gown across the foot of the bed, the pad of someone in slippers going down the hall to the bathroom, the sag of the mattress, the tap dripping in the corner, sudden light when someone opened the door and then closed it again, and the sound of somebody frankly crying, all of us sniffling, "I want to go home," blubbering for Mum. Oh Mum.

When the War was over and bells could ring again, Nunc or more often Young Nunc would go round the halls in the morning *clang clangety clang clang clang!* ringing the handbell to jerk us all awake, a terrible racket we all learned to ignore, stuffing our heads under our pillows and snuggling down to grab extra time in bed, rushing into our clothes at the last minute, breakfast was at half-past eight and we'd compete to see who could stay in bed longest and still get down to the Dining Hall in time, you'd devise ingenious ways of undressing and arranging your clothes the night before so you could get your vest and shirt and pullover on all at once the tie still looped round the neck with a knot in it all it needed was pulling tight, and your underpants and trousers on all at once, you'd tug on your socks, slip your shoes on you'd kept the laces loose, at least I had, but when Birdie did that once his shoe came off and he tripped, somebody grabbed him on the stairs so he didn't fall, after that even tying his laces didn't seem to slow him down we'd all of us learned to be quick, you'd grab your blazer and shovel your arms in the sleeves as you fled downstairs. You couldn't be late for breakfast, you'd get punished you might even have to do without, you had to be there for saying grace "For what we are about to receive may the Lord make us truly thankful Amen" but we all thought it was cheating to sleep in your socks and underwear, we scorned that that was what ignorant townies or even the Nash kids did, evacuees or worse, dirty, not that there were any of them around any more and not that we knew anything about them anyway they weren't near us, we'd all be in a mad scramble to get our clothes on, all of us leaping out of bed at twenty-five-past when Nunc rang the Second Bell telling us to go out through the Quad to the Dining Hall, or even later, not bothering even to wash, combing your hair with your fingers as you clattered down the cement stairs the first kid leaping down all eight steps at once hands on the metal banisters, getting to breakfast all puffed and red in the face and feeling terrific, we'd wolf our breakfast no matter what it was. In the winter there'd be thick patterns of frost on the inside of the window the lino on the floor freezing cold some of us would pull our clothes into the bed under the covers to get them warmed up especially if you slept under a window, it slowed you down getting dressed but you stayed warm wriggling into your trousers under the blankets and hauling your socks on, that got to be a different kind of game it didn't really make things much better, instead of being a bit cold for a few minutes you ended up a bit warmer with your clothes all twisted round and rucked up you'd see kids going down stairs wriggling about trying to get everything comfortable, poking and tugging at their underwear red in the face trying to run down the Quad at the same time as they tucked their shirt in or tightened their tie. But when I first got to Brewood, and until the War was over, Matron went round the dorms first thing *Come on! Time to get up!* ringing in our ears *Come on! Get out of bed!* she might pull the covers off the bed closest to the door jumping us awake, ten minutes later she poked her head round the door to make sure we were all getting dressed properly *"Don't forget to wash behind your ears! Use your flannel! and lots of soap!"* towels all higgledy-piggledy near the washbasins.

That first day she ushered us down to breakfast in the big echoey Dining Hall showing the way, other kids tearing down the stairs to get past us, shouting to each other, stumbling along sleepily behind us, clatter of boots shuffle of feet, long empty tables big enough so everyone in the School could sit and eat all at once, all 140 of them, not many kids, all of us ranged along both sides of one table, a small table for the Masters at the end of the room where the kitchen was and when the other new kids arrived that afternoon we all felt better, they were the ones feeling lost and shy while we all knew each other and had got lockers already even if we did have to share them, we got one shelf each, in the Billiard Room downstairs, a big room with a fireplace at one end, a couple of sofas and a battered armchair, the lockers all along one wall wooden cupboards really stacked on top of each other all the way to the ceiling, and a few chairs and forms round the walls, in the middle an enormous billiard table with a big green lampshade hanging over a huge expanse of fading dark green cloth cues in a couple of racks on the wall by the window and a wooden scoreboard with sliding brass pointers above the fireplace, and we knew that the Billiard Room was what the Headmaster meant when he talked about the Boys' Common Room. And we already had our names on hooks in the entryway and knew where to go to clean our shoes and where the classrooms were and what times meals were, we all knew you couldn't sit down at the table until grace'd been said, and we all waited to see if one of the new kids'd sit down before grace and get scolded, it'd serve 'em right, yesterday we'd been warned not to sit down until grace'd been said, they should've been here yesterday shouldn't they. And Matron knew our names and we knew each other's names, Matron at the head of what'd be the Junior table, we'd seen the Headmaster at his table at breakfast, sitting with Mrs Bailey and the HouseMaster; they had toast and it was in a proper toast-rack, and marmalade from a proper marmalade-pot, they had a tablecloth and serviettes, a little dish of butter for their toast, and a china teapot with a teacosy and a jug of hot water, and after a bit a uniformed kitchen maid popped quietly in through the door behind High Table with a rack of toast and another jug of hot water to give them seconds. We knew how to find the Croft and where the football fields were and the Changing Rooms. But this was the day nearly all of the boarders came back, and now there'd be close on forty boys, some of them as old as sixteen, where yesterday there had been about ten, and tomorrow would be the first day of Term and all the dayboys would be here as well, lessons would start, they'd all be in here for dinner, only at School except on Sundays most kids'd call it lunch.

It can't have been more than two or at most three weeks later, we'd all settled down after Lights Out, some of the kids were already asleep, that Ron Malpas, he was the senior kid he was supposed to keep us in order, said "Listen! They're going to raid us tonight, get your pillow ready!" and Martin or somebody said "Who is? What d'you mean?" I was wide awake, thinking of Mum and Dad

at home talking quietly or listening to the nine-o'clock news, Phil
and me tucked up in bed *What on earth were they talking about?* A
stifled scuffling noise drifted through the ventilator above my head,
and *Ssssh!* and a quiet giggle and *Ssssh!* again, a door quietly
closing along the corridor the pad of a foot the soft brush of clothes
against a wall and *BLAM!* the door burst open flung back against
Alan's bedside locker the muffled *thud* of the locker against the bed
woke Alan up he'd just dropped off and some kid from the Second
Dorm slammed his pillow into Alan's face, tried to anyway but the
door was in the way a silent bunch of kids from the Second Dorm
boiling their striped pyjamas into the room pillows flailing, down the
room between the rows of beds, soft thumps bashing kids as they
scrambled from under the covers pillow whirling about. Morris West
leapt out of bed and shouted "Get 'em!" and charged at a bunch
of them, pillow flailing *He'd been ready for them!* and some of the
kids on the other side of the dorm ganged up together and charged
with him and drove the kids out, "Chase 'em! Come on, get after
them!" but as you got out of the door there was a whole clump of
them ominously staring back down the corridor at us, big-looking.
We hesitated, Alan Franks said "Don't be daft! It's just pillows!" and
he charged at them, the rest of us crowding behind him narked and
laughing, all of us breathless, feet sclabbering away on the floor
you didn't want to get trodden on bare feet or no, and *Slam!* went
the Second-Dorm door, one of us trapped behind it, Tom Fearnley,
in there with them, a prisoner, bangs and thumps and shouts and
laughing, we couldn't open the door a bed pushed against it too
many kids jammed up against it, you'd push and it'd open an inch
or two and then slam shut *Don't get your fingers caught!* shouting
and thumps, bangs and crashes *Ouch! Gerroff!* the door suddenly
opened but only a bit Tom scrambling as they pushed him out
his face bright red he didn't have his pillow any more he'd lost his
pyjama jacket and we all piled up against the door but we couldn't
budge it, we didn't know what to do it was no good hanging about
here and anyway it was too cold for that, we stood helplessly about
all speechless shifting from foot to foot, quiet peeling sounds of
slightly tacky feet shifting on the cold lino, waiting and someone said
"I dunno about you lot but I'm going back to bed" and we all trooped
back puffing and panting, full of palsied beans, it was no good
there was no way we'd just go back to sleep your heart and breath

pounding away like that, and then there was Fearnley and Franks and West going out the door to see if they could raid the Second Dorm back and get his pillow and we all watched and wondered, sitting up in bed all on edge except Gravette, he'd rolled his blankets round him pulled his pillow over his head "Quit it!" he said, "No! I want to go to sleep!" We couldn't hear anything at all from the corridor, not a sound, then the soft scrape of a pillow or a pyjama jacket dragging along the wooden corridor wall, a light footfall and then a shout and a bang, Fearnley and Franks and West going at it like mad and Hart shouted "Come on! Up the First Dorm! Get their mattresses! Grab their clothes!" and we were off, even Gravette's lanky soft body galumphing along behind us and suddenly there's Alan flailing back towards us, Morris and Tom scrambling along, all of us in full retreat *Watch out! they've put shoes in their pillowcases!* to the safety of the dorm.

I thought of a pillowcase swung round the head and then *WHAM!* a shoe in it, that'd knock you flying, the noise was terrific, and what about your teeth, *oh no!* so I scrambled under the bed Alan somehow closed the door I clung to my mattress nobody was going to steal *that*, other kids flailing around me in their pyjamas so close together they couldn't really get a hefty whack in and I just hid all out of breath thinking about shoes and the door swung open, the sound of shoeleather on lino the light clicked on. Along under the beds a pair of pressed grey flannel trousers just above ankle level polished black shoes just inside the door. "What's going on here? You! Stop that!" as Fearnley swung a pillow he'd somehow stolen from the Second Dorm, he couldn't stop the swing his face blank as sudden silence, complete and motionless, breathless, a consternation, one quick loud panting breath a gasp a muffled furtive clump as was it Malpas lowered his pillowcase *had he put a shoe in **his**?* behind him, sheets stripped off beds tangled and messed, dressing-gowns jumbled topsy-turvy, shoes all over the place, clothes scattered everywhere, one pair of bare feet scampering down to the Second Dorm. I peered out, I slowly stood up hoping not to be seen, my bed a shambles. An appalled silence.

Mr Bailey.

There were only supposed to be eight of us, and all in bed, all fast asleep, but there were over a dozen, tousle-haired and sweaty-red, panting and shocked, some of us in only half of our pyjamas, everyone crestfallen looking guilty, not daring even to lift their feet, pillowcases clumping to the floor, but there was nothing you could say. A panic-stricken "Nicks!" from down the corridor, "It's Mr Bailey!" the sound of climbing into bed in Second Dorm, creaks, cautious whispers, light clicking out. You couldn't say "Nothing Sir" you couldn't say you'd come to find something or to ask about your Prep, that would be daftly idiotic even if you could think of it. There was no possible excuse, how could you say you were going to the lavatory, that was the only reason to be out of bed; no one had an excuse, and into that awful silence he said "Gravette! Go to my Study. Hanging on the wall behind the door you'll find my cane. Bring it!" "Oh no uncle," Gravette said, and we all looked at him. *Uncle?* "Please," said Gravette. "Please, uncle." "Fetch it! At Once!" Gravette didn't even put his slippers on, didn't dare. "You other boys go back to your own dormitory. I'll see to you when I'm finished here." And there we all were. "Line up," he said, "Smaller ones first." And then, "No. Malpas. You first: " – pointing to Ron – "In your position you should know better. Put your hands on this chest of drawers," he said, "flat. And bend over." I was littlest but somehow I came third, and Ron walked up as we shuffled into position, a whole line of kids in front of the chest of drawers "Stand back to give room, boy!" Mr Bailey said. "Mind my back-swing!" and Ron bent over as Mr Bailey flexed his cane with its tip in his left hand. It looked just like the ones in the comics, thin and whippy and pale yellow the colour of straw with a curved hook of a handle nestling firmly round his hand, and he said "Straighten your legs child, don't slouch!" and Ron straightened an abrupt tight little upward hump and a sharp thin *Whack!* you could hear the cane singing in the air and *Whack!* and Ron flinched a little jerk I grimaced and as he recovered the cane came down again and then again. We watched Ron as he straightened up his face as red as red could be, blinking like mad his hands at his sides. "Get into bed, boy. Next!" Waiting was a sickish trembling sweat, standing there in line in your pyjamas knowing you were for it, but Ron had stood up straight, like in the Army, and hadn't made a sound, so did the next, so I did too, you had to be brave, *Bend over!* and the evenly-paced *Whack! Whack! Whack! Whack!* left ridges across the bum, great welts, one just at the top of my right leg, the tip of the cane whipped round you, flicked like a bite, *unnngh*, hard into the skin, sharp needle's slap and you waited for the next, that really hurt, *slap!, slap!,* much fiercer than the whacking on your buttocks and you bit back tears and blinked and didn't rub your bum until you got into bed you didn't dare, what would the others think, your rear end wide awake, tingling, near and you were proud you didn't cry, choking it back. But when it got to his turn Gravette started to cry and said "No, uncle, no!" before he'd even got there and cried aloud, bawled and snivelled his way back to bed rubbing his bum and crying out again his snotty face and we all turned our backs on him, such a baby. What had being his uncle got to do with anything.

"Gravette *cried!*" we said next day to everyone as they stood around wanting to hear all about it, and we sneered at him. But Shag Callahan or one of the other Prefects said, when he heard, that he wasn't surprised Gravette'd cried. "Pussy hit him harder than the rest of you, didn't he? Bound to've done, he can't show favouritism, and Pussy *is* his uncle." And that rankled too, what a twerp for not telling us that! But Shag hadn't known that either, till we told him. "No," Shag said, "don't be so silly. What would you think of some kid if he came up and said to you Pussy was his uncle? Putting on side like that?" But what a cissy for crying. "Oh stop it," he said, "you kids are hopeless! Think what it'd be like if you were in his shoes! You'd do the same. Leave it be." But we didn't, of course, and as I look back now, thinking of him as I write this, his perhaps astonished fearful cry *No, Uncle!,* I wonder that I never felt ashamed of the way we treated him, paying him no attention, refusing to be friends. We never learned anything about him, where he lived or what his dad did, he might have been in the Army or something, not that we ever talked about private things like home and family; he might even have been killed in the War, and after that Term we never saw him again, he went to some other school and none of us asked where he'd gone. But of course next day he must have hurt just as much as the rest of us, and most of us spent a lot of the next day standing up. I know I did, rubbing myself tenderly, on a radiator if I could for its warm comfort, the wooden chairs and desks so hard, and one of the dayboys smirked a bit and said the best thing to do if you're going to get whacked is stuff a few sheets of blotting paper down your trousers, "You can hear ordinary paper," he said, "it echoes, and he makes you take it out and then he whacks you again, only harder. And a book's no good you can see it." I only ever got caned again once, it must have been five years later, Mr Bailey long gone, it was with Broggie, I didn't have the chance to pad my behind then, either.

I can still conjure that terrible panicky helpless feeling when I knew it was coming up, not so much my stomach plunging down to my feet as a great wave flooding up through me from the floor, my stomach tottering, my legs not doing what I wanted shaky no longer mine, my lips blurry I didn't dare even try to speak open my mouth, a detached numbness almost taking over not really me not there, mouth dry, sweaty palms, sphincter edgy, eyes unfocussed can't look at anything as they wander, but the floor steady through it all, and the wall, the firmness all outside. Allen Fisher in 2003 told me that he got caned sometime around 1960, at Battersea Grammar School which for some reason had moved to Tooting Bec, because he got caught reading Jack Kerouac's *The Subterraneans*, he'd borrowed it from the public library, and I think that's a pretty monstrous thing to do to a kid, whack him for reading a book, especially a book like that, about on a par with Basil Bunting in 1916 or so almost getting expelled from school when one of the teachers came across him one Sunday crossing out all the unnecessary words in Shakespeare's sonnets, he confiscated the book, but I can't think that Ken and Taffy and me were anything like that enterprising and imaginative. Broggie hardly ever caned anybody, you had to do something really really wrong like when Jeremy Ascough it must've been a couple of years after the War climbed out of the Third Dorm window way after we'd all gone to bed and scampered across the roof and rang the School bell *clang! clang! clang!* in the middle of the night, he must've rung it for a good minute and then scarpered back across the roof and back into bed, he'd hardly got there when the dorm door opened and Broggie walked in flicked the lights on made all of us quake and simply said "Ascough! See me in my study in the morning. After breakfast" and walked out again, didn't say another word *How did he know?* and after he'd left one of us went to the bog and Second Dorm was full of it everyone talking away in admiration, Derek Leigh said that if he'd known ahead of time what Jeremy was thinking of doing he'd've paid him ten bob on a Dare to do it, he was senior to us, "Oh yeah, saved some money didn't 'e?" somebody said when he heard that, but we all admired Derek for that, a little shock of guilty pleasure in Jeremy's heroism and such extravagant approval.

With Ken Hatton and Taffy Evans and me, we'd probably been caught out-of-bounds or taunting Nunc or something as

ordinary as that but persistent. Broggie announced after Prayers
that we'd to come to his Study immediately, we knew we were in for
it. When we got there he told us he would have to cane us, and told
Ken to come in and shut the door, the sound of Broggie's voice with
me and Taffy stood outside listening to the *Whack! Whack! Whack!*
as Broggie administered six of the best. A brief silence, the murmur
of voices. Then the door opening, Ken, blond hair falling over the
side of his red face. We didn't look at each other, and it was my
turn. Broggie standing there with his cane in his hand, it wasn't like
Pussy Bailey's it was heavier, dark brown, but just as whippy, and he
said "Bend over that chair. Lift the tail of your jacket clear," and after
he'd given me six, all evenly spaced, well aimed as well as timed,
I didn't make a sound and nor had Ken, he said "Stand up" in an
indifferent sort of neutral voice and reached across his desk, picked
up a box of chocolates and said "Well taken!" and he smiled. "You
deserve a chocolate," me blinking the welling moisture, catching my
breath, wanting to get out of there fast. Cadbury's *Dairy Box* brand
new, one chocolate gone, I didn't notice which I chose I just took one
I was so astonished, anxious to get through the door said *thank you*
in a strangled sort of voice, and "Yes, Sir," he opened the door and
I left. I didn't look at Taffy but just left, my awkward walk. Ken was
nowhere around I didn't want to see him anyway, not yet, went and
washed my face could feel the welts through my trousers. None of us
talked about it together, not then nor ever, just shoved it to the back
of the mind. It was nothing to talk about, really, except somebody
said, nod of fellow-feeling, one of those kids who was always getting
whacked or so it looked to us, "Did 'e give you a chocolate?"

There really wasn't very much caning and with Mr Bailey it
was hard to tell what you would get caned for, it had to be a terrible
misdemeanour. With only the Headmaster or if necessary the
Assistant Headmaster allowed to do it it existed more as deterrence
than as punishment, and at the same time it invested Mr Bailey with
great Authority, he never spent any time with the boys, mostly left
us to our own devices, we had no idea what sort of bloke he was,
he was remote especially to us young ones but nobody wanted to
be drawn to his attention, and you certainly didn't want to invite his

disapproval. But getting whacked for that dormitory raid in the first Term didn't stop us from having a Midnight Feast in the third, though we were terribly careful about it, we didn't want to get whacked again. I've no idea how it came up, but we all knew about Midnight Feasts, we'd read descriptions of them in places like Billy Bunter books and comics like *Hotspur*, now and again some uncle or family friend who hadn't seen you for a while on being told you were going to Boarding School would smile jovially and ask "Had many Midnight Feasts yet?" or tell us "That's what you do in dormitories," and follow it up with a "Don't get caught or you won't half get into trouble!" but they made it sound like an adventure, and one night in the third Term, it can't have been a weekend night unless it was a Sunday because Willy Pratt was there, he went home every weekend, and he brought the potato crisps, a whole tin full of packets of crisps, his dad owned a factory in Wolverhampton, and he sent along a whole case of orange pop as well, twelve bottles of it in a wooden case, smuggled it upstairs somehow, p'raps his dad helped when he brought him back to School in the delivery van and carried it up himself, Willy put all of it under his bed shoved up against the wall, being a weekly boarder he didn't have a trunk at the foot of his bed. We'd all of us saved our pocket money, every Wednesday after lunch we'd go to Mr Bailey's Study and he'd give us thruppence for the week, older boys got sixpence, and enter it in a book, I thought it was so he'd know he'd given it us but Our Kid said it was so he could send Mum and Dad the bill, just like there was a 1/1d. item on the Term bill, a penny a week for the Church collection but I never knew about that till Mike Blackman wrote me about it when he lent me an old School Magazine in 2001, "One-and-a-penny gravely recorded in the accounts at the end of every Term," he laughed, "church collection." Jimmy Osborne'd told him I was writing this, it never occurred to me that Mum and Dad had to pay for everything and Dad never showed us any of the bills, or talked about them or about money, none of our business, and I never thought about it really till just now, didn't even take it for granted. I knew about the pocket money of course, because some kids got a shilling, their parents had arranged that with the Headmaster, that was a huge amount of money.

We saved up our pocket money for weeks, along with our sweet coupons, and we kept coming back again and again to what

we should get and how much it would cost, and every now and then
somebody would remember something we'd all forgotten, like *do
we need plates*, or *what'll we drink out of*? Harry's mum told him we
should keep it simple, *You don't need plates, how're you going to
wash them up? Use a page out of your notebook! or just use your
notebook. Smuggle stuff out of the Dining Hall. You can't have jelly
or tinned fruit – if you're lucky enough to find some! – nothing like
that* but somebody said he could try and get some sausage rolls
from the butcher shop in the village, that'd be Fatty Gwilt's dad, and
when it came time for the Feast it turned out we'd all got a terrific lot
of stuff, piles of it. Ron and Tom and I had stood outside the baker's
window for ages that day after school eying the cakes in the window
worrying over how much they cost and what kind to get, Tom wanted
a chocolate Swiss Roll and I wanted one with cream and jam in it,
it wasn't real cream of course not in the War, but I liked it anyway I
loved that mix of tastes and textures especially if it was raspberry
jam, and Ron had his eye on what he called a French sponge, and
while we were mucking about trying to make our minds up somebody
from the village went in and bought the chocolate one, it was the last
there was. "Here," Tom said, "we'd better get cracking or we won't
get anything!" so we tossed for it, I said *heads* and it came up tails
so we went in and asked for the French Sponge, the woman gave us
a smile as we took off our School caps and asked about the cake,
she said "Somebody's birthday, is it?" and I said "No" just as Tom
said "Yes" and he gave me a look and I went red, and she smiled
again, real amused, and said only it was almost a whisper as she
leaned forward "Are you planning a midnight feast then?" We didn't
know what to say to that, but Ron pulled himself up a bit and looked
out the door, gave a bit of a nod without really giving it away and she
said "I wonder if I can find a box for it" and went into the back.

   And of course after Lights Out it was impossible to go
to sleep, we were all obviously excited when Matron came to
turn off the light she must have known something was up, all
the toothbrushes nice and tidy by the washbasins, and all the
spongebags hanging up where they were supposed to be, not the
way they usually were. "Have you washed behind your ears?" she
asked and looked round at all of us, she was much more particular
than usual, me and I expect everyone else praying like mad she
wouldn't get it into her head to have a look under Pratt's bed

where all those bottles of pop were, he'd moved the potato crisps to his locker they hardly fit in there were so many packets terrible crumpling noise as he pushed them in *I hope they didn't break to smithereens* and she went over to Blondie's bed and then turned away and tugged at Harry's ears in the next bed over to have a look and he just squirmed a bit and said "Ow" and "Yes, Miss, I really scrubbed them" and she asked "Whose flannel is this on the floor? Hang it up. Be quick about it!" and somebody or other got out of bed and did what she said. The rest of us all just lay there in bed shifting about a bit all restless and impatient, nobody saying anything unless he was talked to, all the usual chatter just gone, everyone quiet, and she gave us a look as she went to the door and said "You make sure you go to sleep now!" and smiled round the room, "No mischief!" and turned the light out. "Good night, boys!"

After we chorused our reply none of us said anything, not like other nights when we'd usually gossip and chatter a bit or play some sort of word game for a while before settling down. We just lay there staring at the patches of light shining on the ceiling through the ventilator, and after a while somebody said "What time is it?" and somebody else said "The Third Dorm hasn't come up yet." They didn't have to go to bed till half-past eight, you could hear them talking away in the Billiard Room which was right underneath us, and we just lay there waiting and waiting, how long were they going to be? A hoarse whisper, "Hey Pratt, chuck us a packet of crisps," and we had a furtive whispered argument about how we couldn't start yet, somebody said "Did anybody bring a knife" and a small chorus of voices said to a lot of *sssssh*ing that they'd pinched one from the Dining Hall. Blondie Hart said in an almost ordinary tone of voice "Hey, you lot, keep it quiet! My Dad says whispering carries for miles! Just speak in a low voice" and Birdie said "Yeh, it'll sound like Ron snoring!" and we all giggled, "they won't notice that!" We just lay there and lay there and Harry said "I don't know how she missed it, but I left my knife on my locker, she must've seen it, I bet she knows what we're doing" but Blondie said "your locker's always such a mess nobody'd ever see anything on it. Your snot rag's still there, I can see it!" and somebody giggled, "Going to cut the cake with a snotty knife?" and we all chortled a bit, even Harry. And then we just lay there and lay there, we lay there forever, and at last a door opened downstairs voices suddenly louder, a laugh or two,

"Come on, hurry up! It's bedtime," a door closed, clatter of shoes, feet and talk coming up the cement stairs, the patch of light on the ceiling suddenly sharp and bright as a light turned on, chatters and mutterings and the sound of running water and the bright patch on the ceiling turned pale, the Third Dorm slow settling into the night, quiet, the Fourth and Fifth Dorms coming up ten minutes later, quieter, and a tiny whisper from the corner *Red leather yellow leather red leather yellow leather* "Who's that?" A hissed *shurrup you fool!* "I'm just trying to pass the time, do you know any tongue-twisters?" A bed creaking as someone turns over and a quiet voice said "Hey, that's not a bad idea. D'you know this one? Shut up the shutters and sit in the shop?" a quiet gurgle, *w-h-a-a-t?* and what popped into my head was *Polish it behind the door,* I giggled, a faint susurrus of whispering round me and a voice from the corridor, "You boys go to sleep! It's ten o'clock!" *It's Matron!* and Willy Pratt said in a sleepy-sounding voice, bless his heart, "Yes Miss" with a loud yawn. And we just lay there tossing about, Martin said "I bet it's not ten o'clock, nothing like!" and we lay there and lay there and lay there all this bubbling up going on inside, how could you sleep with all that glee.

Wait.

Wait.

And wait some more. Lie on your stomach, listen to the wind in the monkey-puzzle tree, lie on your back, roll over, hang your arm over the edge of the bed, wonder why the window's rattling, pummel your pillow, back on your stomach again, swing your arm back and forth trying to reach the floor, yawn, turn over. Somebody walking down the corridor, a light at last clicking off outside, just a dim glow through the ventilator, drifting off, nice snuggled up *mustn't go to sleep,* warm blanket tucked round my ears, quiet, dark. And *Ouch! Gerroff!* big rustle of paper *What d'you think you're doing?* and there was Harry clambering about on Alan's bed, frantic whispers, *Hold me up, Alan!* standing on the bedstead reaching up, crackle of stiff paper, Blondie flashing a torch in their direction *Point it at the floor you booby!* and I could see Harry pinning a big sheet of paper over the ventilator, he'd brought it from art class, "Watch out!" he said, "I dropped a drawing pin" and "Hope it's not in my bed" Alan said, somebody giggled, and there were Ron and Tom covering the other ventilator. *Alright, it's OK now!* that was Willy, *We can start now,* a flurry of activity and giggles and murmurs as we pulled our tartan

rugs off our beds and spread them on the floor, three or four torches
going, mine so feeble there was just a faint glow, the bike shop
in the Square hadn't had any batteries they were always in short
supply and even if you could find one they cost a lot, rustling sounds,
bumps *Here, give us a knife!* crinkle of crisp packets suddenly loud
as somebody undid the twist of salt and shook the packet to spread
it about, *hey! not so loud!* all of us fidgeting away half-on half-off our
rugs trying to keep clear of the cold lino, dressing gowns dragging
and drooping as you hunted your socks out, draggy scraping noise
as Willy hauled the pop from under his bed, clink of pop bottles,
Blimey! 'Oo's got an opener scuffling sound of Alan coming up with
his fancy knife it'd got everything on it, scissors, nailfile, screw-driver,
corkscrew, pig-sticker, three blades, it was a smashing knife, even a
bottle-opener, "Made in Switzerland," he'd told us proudly, "My Dad
got it when he went there before the War," gurgle of pop being drunk.
All of us just munching away, all of us on edge, listening for noises
from outside, and Harry as usual stirring about and restless. He
suddenly said "Hey did you hear this joke? It was in the *Beano*" and
as he said it we heard a door close, *Nicks!* we all froze, off went the
torches, you didn't dare breathe, a bit of cake halfway to my mouth,
my hand poised in midair, what good that'd've done if anybody'd
come in I didn't know, the bog flushed, a door opened, footsteps
down the corridor towards the Third Dorm, bare feet not slippers,
mutter of a deep voice, a door closing again, and we all breathed
a bit. A soft clatter followed by a quiet *glug* and then another, and
Birdie said *Oh no!* quite loud, he'd knocked his pop over, he was a
really fastidious kid, always looked neat, it'd spilled all across his rug,
and Harry got up he was closest to the washbasins and threw him
a towel "That'd better not be mine" Tom said as Birdie tried to mop
it up. "I'll rinse it out," he told him "you can use mine tomorrow," but
whose was it? I felt a bit disgruntled about that, we none of us used
each other's towels, that was like using each other's toothbrushes
or wearing somebody else's dirty underwear, and in the middle of a
chuckle Willy yawned *I wonder what time it is.* Martin peered at his
watch in the gloom, he was the only one of us had one, and then
"'Alf a mo'," he said. "No, give us a bit of light" and as he looked he
leaned back, a small crunch behind him as he sat on a bunch of
lady-fingers, crumbly dry powder all over the rug next his bum, and
then "I dunno, I think it must've stopped," and he held it to his ear,

"No, it's still ticking. It's just after twelve" and we couldn't believe it, it was hardly even midnight, some kids' parents wouldn't've gone to bed yet. My bum was getting a bit numb from sitting on the floor and I looked round at the others, there were crisp packets and bottle caps and empty bottles and bits of paper and cutlery, crumbs and broken ladyfingers and stuff all over the place, there was a sausage roll over by Birdie's foot, someone'd contrived to get some, and us without ration books, who managed that I wonder *Crikey! We'll have to clean all this up before we go to bed* and suddenly I gave a great big yawn and stretched my arms out, Birdie looked at Willy and Blondie said "I think I'm going to sleep" and as we gathered up our rugs to put them back on our beds munching at bits and pieces of stuff as we cleared up there was a loud clatter as a couple of knives and a full bottle of pop fell to the floor and we froze, all the torches off, listening, proud sort of giggle bubbling up barely held down, my heart pounding away my mouth chock full of sausage roll and my feet getting colder and colder. *Okay,* somebody whispered, I took a quick swig to get it down, and Ron turned his torch back on, rushed sleepy exhilaration, we stuffed all the rubbish any old how into our lockers, frantic that we'd been heard yet wanting to chirp. The floor was cold, and so was I.

In the morning Matron just banged on the door and opened it a bit to get us up, she didn't even stick her head round the door, *Come on! Rise and shine! We're a bit late this morning! You'll have to hurry even if you* are *tired!* and there was a big sticky patch in the middle of the floor where Birdie had spilled his pop. There were still bits of crisp packets and stuff all over the place, mostly under the beds. "Hey!" Willy said, "look!" and he held up three twists of blue paper, one of them open, "I've got salt all over my bottom sheet!" and we laughed, but the floor when I got out of bed was all gritty too, salt and crisp crumbs sticking to my feet. "That's it!" Alan said, "That's enough adventure for me!" but he grinned as he flinched his feet across the room to the washbasins, his slippers in his hands. "I'm going to wash my feet before I put anything on them! I don't want to walk about on salt and crisps all day, get it in my socks and shoes" and while some of us washed, the rest of us scurried about trying to tidy everything up *We should do it again* we said, it was a terrible mess really even after we'd finished, we didn't have a dustpan or a broom or anything like that, and Birdie picked up his tartan rug and grimaced it was all soggy and sticky at one end, "I'll wash it after breakfast" he said, and we shrugged. We were all a bit droopy after too little sleep, and everything felt strange, the room was different now, it was really ours. And at Breakfast Mrs Grant looked us over, and said "Smithe, you look as though you've been dragged through a hedge backwards" and Martin came over all innocent, "I know you boys have been up to something, I don't want to know what, but you'd better not get caught, and you'd better pull your socks up or you'll get in trouble," and up at High Table the HouseMaster gave us a sidelong glance and Mr and Mrs Bailey studiously ignored us. We all grinned and felt a bit sheepish, pure little lambs, and she laughed. "It's a good thing it's me," she said as a murmur drifted over from High Table, "and not a Prefect, who gets you up in the morning. But don't take advantage!"

When I'd first arrived at Brewood, ages ago, that very first morning in September, somebody had said at breakfast in a loud voice that the junior boys had to fag for the Seniors and especially for the Prefects, "Didn't you know?" and "You'd better not get Russell, he does terrible things to his fags" but he wouldn't say what, and told us that the small room just inside the boarders' entrance on the right we all had to pass it on the way in or out of the building was the Prefects' Sitting Room, you didn't want to get caught in there with the door closed and they had a fire lit, and I had visions of Flashman bullying his way through *Tom Brown's Schooldays*, would they burn you, did they torture just for fun – or for any reason – but somebody else whispered "Don't be daft, he's just joking. You're too small anyway," and next day Brian Holland, a New Boy in the Third Form, he'd be about ten or even perhaps eleven, older than me by quite a bit, was sent by a Prefect to get a bottle of pop from Mrs Roberts's tuck shop just down the road from the Gates. And that was all. After that nobody did any fagging for anyone, nobody forced anybody else to make his bed for him or clean his shoes or get coal for the fireplace or pinch some extra bread from the Dining Hall so they could make toast or mend a puncture on their bike or anything like that, fagging just died out as a practice if it ever was one, but I wasn't the only kid whose vague sense of dread made him sneak past that door, I never even dared glimpse inside if it was even half-open, and we'd all read too much about Prefects and bullies in stories about Greyfriars or Dotheboys Hall, and knew it went on in other schools. So it was a great relief early in the Term when Matron told us in the dorm, at bed time, "Don't worry about it, Fagging doesn't happen here at all, it's not allowed at all, and don't you let anybody try it on, they'll get punished if they do. We've put a stop to that." One way or another though a bit of bullying went on, bigger kids forcing younger ones to hand over half their sweet ration and things like that, or small ones just getting caught by themselves in a Cloakroom or in the Changing Room or even just somewhere outside, out by the Croft or in the Spinney or over on the playing fields, and being punched about a bit and made to do things by bigger boys we didn't know what. But if anything like that happened you just had to take it, you didn't dare tell anyone, you couldn't report it to a Master or to any grown-up, it'd just make the bully worse. So you put up with it and kept your mouth shut.

A bunch of us'd be standing around over by School Bridge above the canal or playing some game in a corner of the Croft or clattering about in Big School, and I'd see this kid walking round the edge of the field back towards the dormitory avoiding everybody, or going along the border of the drive towards the Gates, hunched-up shoulders crumped over not looking at anyone, one of us'd look over at him, a quick little glance really, over his shoulder, *There goes Neville* said real quiet, a mutter more to himself than to the rest of us, and our talk'd falter a bit or there'd be a little pause in play or in talk as you tried not to see him, absolutely not to stare, but you couldn't help looking, you'd cast a quick little flash, your eyelids pressing up against your brow as you lowered your head you didn't want him to know you were looking, but of course he did, sometimes on your Sunday Walk you'd see Neville in his grey shorts and blazer faltering out of the woods across the field away from the shadowy figure of a bigger kid back under the trees you couldn't tell who, just a dark menacing shape, and I'd avert my gaze and steer my walk away from the small figure drooping back towards the School. The first time that happened I looked out across the field and said "Who's that? What's he doing over there?" and Fred or somebody turned round on me, fast, and said "Sssssh! Shurrup, don't draw his attention! you don't want him to notice us" as the shadowy disturbing figure way over the field turned back toward the trees. You never said a word to the poor kid or asked him anything, none of us did anything. Sometimes on a half-day or a Sunday somebody a year or two older than you would quietly say "There he goes again, poor kid" and there he'd be, trudging across the Croft or up Dirty Lane by himself. At first I didn't understand at all, but one day somebody quietly said "Predder's over there already" and looked towards that shadowy large figure. Nobody said anything, and for a long time I didn't know who they were talking about, that wasn't anyone's nickname that I knew. I was always afraid to talk to Neville, I couldn't go over to him as he walked along in his misery he was so different from the rest of us and on any other day I wouldn't know what to say to him anyway, it was difficult to meet his eye, and to this day I don't know whose gaze slid off first, his or mine, there was an embarrassment somewhere in the weakness we found in his wretchedness.

I'd been at Brewood for a couple of years or even more before I really began to notice something was going on and we none of us thought the Masters knew at all. Our Kid told me on the phone when we were talking about bullies and life at Brewood that when Brian Harley, he got to be Professor of Geography at the University of Wisconsin and was the same age as Our Kid, they were in the same Form but I don't remember him at all, Phil says he was quite a small lad, when Brian Harley died in 1991 his friend Paul Laxton in the *Independent* talked about the "miserable treatment" Harley'd had at Brewood, and I wrote away and got a copy. What an "easy target" he must've been, Laxton wrote, "a country boy in hand-me-down clothes but with a sharp intellect." His parents didn't have much money, "impecunious" Laxton calls them, and they weren't even his mum and dad really, they were just foster parents, the other kids'd certainly hold that against him especially if he had any brains, he wasn't like the rest of us, and another obituary in the *Times* said a bit pompously that he was "pre-disposed to champion the cause of those deprived and dispossessed by the establishment, whether of state, church, or social class," and implied that his work on maps was as important as it was because he spoke "not only from what was in his fertile mind but also from the heart." When I was in my forties one of my colleagues in the English department talked in a meeting about the necessity for what he called "blooding" graduate students, I expect he had something like what we did to Birdie Prince in mind, giving them a hard time with impossible exams and hostile orals, *you've got to test them under fire*, he said, *make them think under pressure*, and there he was, Predder the bully all over again but smugly self-satisfied, shoving something or other down people's throats, terrorizing. Small wonder, later on, that jolt of recognition reading *Great Expectations*, Pip screwed down so hard by Mrs Joe and that ass Pumblechook and then Estella.

But Our Kid and me were probably lucky; I know I was. A couple of days after School first started I walked into the Billiard Room, I had steel tips on the heels of my shoes so they wouldn't wear out so fast, *clink-clunk clink-clunk clink-clunk* really loud on the tile floor outside the door, one of them a bit loose, and this really big kid in a brown jacket, much older than me he could have been one of the Teachers almost, stuck out his arm as I went in and said "You've got a heavy tread for somebody so small! What's your name?" and my voice got all wavery I couldn't tell he if he was friendly or not and I told him and he said "How old are you?" and the other boys at that end of the room stopped talking and I told him and he said "You must be the Youngest Boy, then" and I said "Yes," I was about a year younger than the next youngest in the whole School, proud of the distinction but bothered too, there were other people listening the whole room had gone quiet everyone was looking and he said "Your brother's Phil isn't he?" and I said "Yes" and he said "Then you're Little Phil, aren't you!" and turned away dismissing me but I didn't know it to talk to somebody next to him, another big kid carving away at a piece of wood with a big clasp knife. I just stood there wondering what to do and a voice from the other side of the room said "Hey Little Phil come over here!" and somebody laughed. I went all round the billiard table keeping well away from someone leaning over the table to take a shot, he'd waited while I'd been quizzed perhaps he wanted to see what'd happen, and the name stuck, it would be a while before I got called Scat instead, and this kid said "Do you know who that was?" and I said "No" worrying I'd done something wrong, everybody around listening, and he said "That's Fatty Bullimore, he can beat anybody in the School except Bud Flanagan, that's who he's talking to" and I worried some more, and this kid said "You'll be alright, then," meaning that Fatty had taken me under his wing, and he was right, Fatty was a gentle bloke, but I didn't see that then, and for a couple of years I was protected. Until Fatty Bullimore left, nobody dared bully me, at least not often. I'd get into fights, of course, kids always do, and I couldn't go twitting off to Fatty for anything like that, I couldn't go twitting off to Fatty at all anyway wrong or right but there was no need to, everybody knew Fatty had called me Little Phil, I'd got my nickname as easily as that. But I couldn't put on any side, you couldn't go twitting anyway, kids didn't tell on other kids, not to the Masters nor to older kids, you always shouted *Nicks!* if there was a Master coming, whether anybody was doing something wrong or not we all stuck together, you had to warn the other kids let them know there was an adult around, or even a Prefect, and it was always funny to read that in other schools like ours, schools like Greyfriars or Dotheboys, kids called *Cavey!* as though that was the proper word for *Nicks!* We knew better and thought they were a bit cissy. We never queried such things, any more than we wondered why the Quad was called the Quad, we knew it stood for Quadrangle, but it was nothing like one really, it was just a sort-of oblong shape with two or three arms sticking out if you made a map of it, not a bit like the Quad of an Oxford college or in *Tom Brown's Schooldays*, it wasn't square at all the sides and ends weren't parallel, and it was years before I thought about it enough to realise that *Nicks* was really *Nix* and was Latin, like *Cave*, some sort of holdover from the time when everybody learned Latin and smaller boys were ruled by older boys and subject to their every whim. You couldn't let the Masters discover what you were doing because they might stop it.

I found out soon enough that that meant you had to fight your own battles, someone like Fatty couldn't protect you from everything, didn't want to, you wouldn't want him to either. Even that very first night in the dorm, Gravette snivelling away me wanting my Teddy-bear, I just knew everybody'd mock if you had a Teddy-bear at School, of course looking back now I haven't any real idea whether that's true but none of the other kids'd brought theirs, you didn't dare even ask if they'd got one, you knew you'd probably pretend you didn't have one yourself if anyone asked, *what're they asking for?* Gravette was the only one who'd brought any fancy toys that you knew about, of course we'd all got a couple of dinky toys but only the little ones you could put in your pocket, cars or perhaps a model destroyer or spitfire, none of the big fancy things like lorries or Wimpeys they were far too precious. When everybody got back to School you found out some of the older kids had brought things like Meccano sets and Totopoly, things with lots of pieces, they kept them in their lockers, games and toys like that were sacred, they really did belong to someone, you might've wished you'd got one yourself the way much later on we all wished we had Robin Rawlings's game of *Dennis Wheatley's Invasion!* that was obsessive, we'd play it for hours and hours, no one fooled about stealing them, or hiding them; like jigsaw puzzles, lose a piece of them and you were all losers. But Teddy-bears were fair game, they wouldn't last long at School. Nobody'd protect you if somebody snitched a Teddy-bear and kicked it about in the mud or played pig-in-the-middle with it, Bullimore couldn't protect you from that nor could anybody else, you just knew that without being told. Poor Graham Harvey, one morning at Break a pair of kids came up while he was playing with a couple of Dinky Toys on the tarmac in a corner of the Quad and helped themselves, took them off him, we all knew he'd get them back when Break was over though he might have to scramble for them a bit they weren't *thieves*. They started jeering at him for playing by himself they'd got his toys, he started shouting, lost his temper, flew at one of them and then there was a fight, Graham and one of the kids, and we all gathered round and started shouting the way kids do, a Master came up *What's going on? Stop this fight!* and we all fell silent. *What's this all about?* and Graham said "Please Sir they took my Dinky Toys when I was playing with them," and after the Master broke it up and had gone away we all stood in a circle round Graham and chanted at him "Twit! twit! twit! twit! twit!" I was shouting with the rest "Twit! twit! twit! twit! twit! twit! twit!" louder and louder insistent heavy beat "Twit! twit! twit! twit! twit! twit! twit! twit! twit! twit!" until he cried and the Master came back and sent us all away. It was really very frightening, and next day I said "hello" a lot of us did but didn't know what to say to him we couldn't meet each other's eyes. He never did get a nickname.

Bud Flanagan was Black Irish, black black hair and blue blue eyes, compact build, didn't speak much to anyone hardly except Fatty that I remember. He was mad about the sea, couldn't wait to leave school so he could join the Merchant Navy, always reading about it, had pictures of ships in his pocket; always carving away at a model. Some evenings, after homework, or in the late afternoon and at weekends, Seniors would get permission to open up the

woodworking shop where there were big workbenches with vices
and racks for woodworking tools, glues and paint and varnishes,
and brushes and different kinds of saws and chisels and drills
and planes, mallets and hammers and screwdrivers in tall lock-up
cupboards one end of the room, you weren't allowed to use any of
them until you'd taken Woodwork so nobody in Prep School could
do any carpentry, I was too small to be allowed to go in at all. In May
1942 when Our Kid was nearly eleven he got into the Third Form
he began taking Woodwork, his Report Book says he was "Shaping
well" and "Shaping nicely," I wonder as I write this what that *shaping*
means, but there was no Woodwork Teacher a year later, in my
Report Book the Woodwork slot never got filled in, the Teacher who'd
gone into the Army in 1940 had been replaced by Mrs Bailey's father
but he was an old man and couldn't do it anymore. I don't remember
him at all, never laid eyes on him so far as I know. So there wasn't
anybody when I got into the Third Form at the beginning of 1944, the
workshop was still there, not much wood left from the supplies laid in
before the War, all the carpentry benches and piles of chairs shoved
to the back of the room, it was just a classroom now, Form IVA, a
couple of the benches still usable if you shifted the desks around,
dusty chains of fluff at the back, scraps of paper, sweet wrappings,
a wood-shaving or two, Nunc never swept there, couldn't get at it.
But Bud Flanagan every so often would get a piece of four-by-four
and rough-cut it with a handsaw into the shape of a boat, following
pencil lines he'd drawn, getting the shape from books in the library,
silhouettes from *Jane's All the World's Merchant Ships* most likely.
After that he'd carve it by hand, at first with a chisel holding the wood
in a vice, but mostly with his clasp knife, he carried it everywhere,
you'd see him sitting quietly in a corner of the Billiard Room whittling
away, sharpening it on his pocket stone, checking his carving with a
pair of dividers from his geometry set, dozens of shouting screaming
kids, sometimes all thirty or forty of us in that room arguing and
laughing and playing, singing and talking, and he'd be carving
away at the hull and then smoothing it down with a bit of sandpaper
or shaping it with a woodfile, and when that was done he'd get
more scraps of wood and carve and build hatches and cabins and
superstructure, tiny hinges and hasps and doorknobs and lamps and
wheels and winches, he'd shave away at bits of dowelling to make
masts and derricks, he'd paint all the parts and glue them together,

nails and thread for deckrails and rigging, portholes scribed into the hull with minuscule rims put round them, cellophane for glass, absolutely exquisite detailed models of merchant ships, everything scrupulously to correct scale, painted in the proper colours, yacht-buff masts, black hulls painted red below the waterline, white superstructure, lines drawn on the deck for planking, stiff shaped-cardboard propellers, rudders that turned, funnels in the proper insignia for the shipping company, and he'd mount it all on a wooden cradle, name on the stern and on the cradle, and stow it carefully somewhere, in his locker, or in a Master's keeping perhaps. Our Kid told me a couple of months ago when I was reading this bit to him over the phone that Bud Flanagan cried his eyes out his last day at School when he was sixteen, I didn't know that at all, but we both knew, so did everyone, that as soon as he got out of school, that was at the end of my first year at Brewood, he was going to join the Merchant Navy and go to sea, quite a few Senior Boys carried around *The Able Seaman's Handbook* wherever they went you'd come across them working their way through it or practicing their knots, I think it cost about sixpence but it was nearly the end of the War before Our Kid got his hands on a copy to buy, and the first morning when we all came back in September 1942 the Headmaster told us all at Prayers in Big School that Bud Flanagan had sailed in a North Atlantic convoy in June, his ship had been torpedoed, and he had drowned. Gaumont British News, "One of Our Convoys," men floundering in oil-slicked water their ship sinking, voice over grainy black-and-white, grimmish music gussying it up, an arm flailing in dark water among lifejackets and lifeboats. There was a notice board near the Masters' Common Room, and now and again a new name would appear.

A.E.Conway, killed in action, North Africa.

Michael Flanagan, missing, North Atlantic.

Mr Bailey would read the names out to us. It didn't happen very often, but someone you knew even if only a little bit, however remote he was from us seven- and eight-year olds, was now dead from the War, or missing in action. Or a Prisoner-of-War. What we'd been reading about in the paper was now here, where we were, in the Billiard Room and in the Quad and in the classroom. With us, and at the same time gone.

We'd have two minutes of silence at School Prayers, and

the formality of it would tell you what you hadn't known. Bud's name was Michael, his nickname from the music hall team of Flanagan and Allen a curious intimacy, *Michael* the estrangement insulating you from shock, him drowning, and I thought of brasswork and glossy paint, his boat models, where they were, what would happen to them. That was about as close as the War would get, out in the Staffordshire countryside, except in early December after Mr Bailey went to prison, that was 1944, I went for the weekend to Robin Salmon's, his dad had a farm out near Uttoxeter at the end of a long lane off a secondary road, miles away from anywhere, much too far to walk to the nearest village if you'd got stuff to carry. Cold drizzle on Saturday afternoon we all piled into their sit-up-and-beg pre-War Austin his mum and dad in the front and us two ten-year-olds in the back, *Get your mac on*, his mum said and looked at my boots and nodded, *Yes, they'll do, wrap up warm*, Robin and I wondered where we were off to. *What we were talking about last night*, she said, *the explosion*. I wasn't any the wiser, but Robin said "A farm blew up, it's gone, it's not there any more" and before I could ask anything else his dad said "It was an arms dump, a big explosion. It's not far away, up at Faulds, we thought we'd have a look," but we kept driving around, the two grown-ups peering through the steamed-up windows trying to find it along unmarked country lanes, some of the landmarks were missing, and at last his Dad said "I know that tree" just as his mum said "There's Whitcombs" so we just parked the car at the gate to a field *It's that way, the old gypsum mine, not far now* and I shivered a bit as we walked in the cold drizzle. "You'll soon warm up," his mum said, but the clamminess of a soggy country lane was not very appealing. It'd all sounded exciting when we started out, but as we got closer I got a bit nervous *Has it all been cleared up? I don't want to see any dead people* and my thoughts shied away from what it'd feel like if I did. *I'll not look*, I decided, but of course I would, you couldn't help looking, the way we all had after an Air Raid in Birmingham earlier on after we'd been allowed out of the shelter, a funny mix of hope and dread, hard to think about even if it was someone you'd never heard of *I've never seen a dead body. Except at the pictures, on the news.* The four of us slowly drifted apart to make a raggedy line across a huge ploughed field, nothing growing, just bare wet dirt, not a sign of any mine or any factory, just mud and small pebbles, grey raggedy scraps that might be concrete, mired stodge, puddles. The furrows went every which way, not really furrows at all, not much in the way of trees or hedges they'd all been flattened, Robin's dad said he'd heard from one of the men that something like three inches of dust had fallen on the whole countryside *a thick blanket* but the rain had settled it, mud built up on my boots, heavy, clinging, when I tried to kick it off it just smeared and clung and spread, got worse and worse, nothing there to scrape it off, not even a stiff twig, utterly useless scraps of wood, my hands getting colder and wetter, my gloves a complete waste of time, rain trickling down my neck, my cap soaked, mud on my mac, puddles and rivulets of water to scramble across, "Not far now," Robin's mum said as I thought *We'll be here forever,* up ahead a handful of people standing at a wire fence where everything had been cordoned off *You can't get any closer,* pointing and talking. Someone said "It's a hell of a crater, it must be half a mile across, they'll be clearing it up for months" and someone else said "It's a hundred yards deep, water at the bottom" but I couldn't believe that. It turned out later it was more like a hundred *feet,* but the thirty-odd yards those feet made still meant a lot of hole, it's called the Hanbury Crater nowadays, more like what you'd see at a quarry but without the lorries and sheds, with that fence keeping us back there really wasn't anything to see, just churned up mud, empty land with a few flattened bits of trees and stuff, no hedges, no buildings, no wreckage, and as we turned to go back Robin drifted off a bit to my left or perhaps it was me to the right we got quite a bit apart and in my squelchy leap across some water to a small steep ridge of mud I looked over to see how he was doing and a rank and foul pungent stink smacked across my face right from my feet as I landed, bits of dark muddy red stuff clinging to a long dirty bone wriggly white bits on it *Are those maggots?* a bit of hairy skin, edges pulled back, maggots again, dark red-black spills staining here and there. I couldn't look but couldn't *not,* and I wanted to cry out but didn't dare, I'd have to show it to the others *Hey, come and look at this!* and talk about it but the choking acridity caustic in my mouth and throat paralysed my tongue and breath, my belly shuddered as I tried to swallow my flooding spit, and in the cold could not, so spat.

    By the time we got back to the car I'd told it anyway, and Robin said he saw it too, "Bet it was a cow leg," he said, "too big to be anything else." And his dad said "Hayes Farm's just *disappeared,*" he said, "just *gone*, not a trace. And the reservoir." His mum said that's where the water came from that made it so muddy, and I wondered. "The whole thing went up last month," she said, "in the morning. We heard it, all these miles away." Lord Haw-Haw had said on the radio from Hamburg that blowing up the arms dump was a great German victory, but none of us believed that, there'd been no V-2 rockets anywhere near us, it'd just happened the way accidents do, and we sat there, thinking about the devastation we hadn't really seen and I was glad I hadn't really seen it. I didn't really know what I felt about it, it was terrible that a whole farm'd been obliterated and everyone in it, the farmer and the field he was in vanished without a trace, but it was so huge that it didn't quite seem real, had nothing to do with the War really, just an accident like a natural disaster, but we didn't talk about it, nobody ever said anything about it in class or at School and when you get right down to it we none of us thought it had anything to do with any of us, after all there was nothing round here that'd make fields and villages just vanish, blown to smithereens.

At the end of morning prayers in Big School a bit over three years later, in May 1948 long after the War was over, School Assembly'd been a bit quieter than usual, we'd finished the hymn and were getting ready to go to class, a Police Inspector, his back ramrod straight and his uniform all sharp creases and his cap square on his head, marched to the middle of the stage, all the Masters still standing without a move, completely erect no smiles or quiet chuckles the way there usually was, Henry Houston as fierce-looking as ever with his ginger hair and red cheeks, the rest unsmiling their gaze levelled straight ahead, and Mr Finney, he'd been Headmaster since April, said "This is Chief Inspector McWilliams from the Staffordshire Police." This was something new. He wasn't even the local bobby. We'd never seen *him* before. And you could cut the silence with a knife, Mr Finney still standing, some kid at the front muttered something and met a hurried *Ssh!* from his neighbour. Nobody relaxed. The Inspector cleared his throat and nodded, and told us in a grave voice that Rex Farran *He's in the class ahead of mine!* had been killed yesterday at home in Codsall when a parcel that he opened exploded *Our Kid knows him*, I thought, and then *No wonder all the kids from Codsall are so quiet.* It was a bomb that'd been sent in the post. "You must all be very careful if you get any parcels or fat letters that you don't expect, especially if you don't know where they're from or who sent them. Whatever you do you *must not* open them, you shouldn't even touch them if you can avoid it, you should leave them alone and report them to the nearest adult. *Don't* go near them for *any* reason, not even to have a look!" And he told us Rex'd opened it by mistake, it'd been addressed to "R. Farran." "It may have been intended for his older brother who has the same initial," he said, and as we were leaving Big School I heard someone say he'd seen Roy Farran around last week, on leave from the Army, "He's an officer in the Palestine Police" somebody else told me, "He's really tough, he's a hard man."

I didn't know what to think about it all, the two Farrans in the School were a bit frightening they were so much bigger than me as well as older, they threw their weight about on the soccer field and just went their own way, I don't think they ever spoke to me at all, not ever, and nobody talked about Rex very much after, he just wasn't there any more, but I overheard Gordon Thwaits, he was in the Sixth Form, tell one of his pals that the bomb'd been sent by the Stern Gang, he'd read it in the paper, but that didn't make me any the wiser, we never talked about it in class, the teachers never said anything at all, and I forgot about Rex pretty soon after. I'm sure if I came from Codsall and was there every day that there'd've been a lot of talk between the grown ups and even between them and the kids, but I suppose while the War was on we all got a bit used to sudden things like that parcel bomb, but not when it'd been over for something like three years. When we were staying with him that summer Uncle Edward said to quite a chorus of tut-tutting that "After all, a bomb-parcel's not as bad as the V-2 was, *that* came right out of the blue, really a terrible explosion straight out of nowhere, with absolutely no warning. A parcel, though, well, that gets delivered by somebody, so there's something to expect, there's a sort of warning." Yet there were a few nods of agreement. It was all very odd. Fatty Gwilt's dad said in his butcher shop in the village that the War came closest to Brewood only after the War was long over. And then he said "But Palestine's a different war," he said, "And it's really got nothing to do with us. Not like Hitler's war."

(chapter 6, from Growing Dumb*)*

Makimonos

Richard Makin

Imagine the outskirts of a vast, futuristic city whose interior is unreachable, for you are consigned forever to its margin, a zone of permanent electrical storms, acid rain and the wreckage of past conceits.

Accepting and encompassing banality – all this is obvious, I know – circumscribing many voices, invited or otherwise. And are you a part of it? Yet at the same time to remember (this is difficult). And the Everlasting Clocks – and the reckoning of the tide, the moon and the stars. And there are films. And there is the wireless, with its pumping, beating valves.

Another, I suppose because it's no longer current, is correspondence with the big, inherited books.

'An organic spaceship: a vast single-cell amoeba,' she adds.

Anything that could be said doubtless has. Are there any unhelpful ways to read? Are there models, however remote, that we can point to as being analogous? As for writers, they all touch different nerves.

Basically, the whole cave gets taken over. (Say that again.) It was like being tonguetied. Bracketed words seem to release tension, changing tack when a change of tack is needed – but yes, flowers for the dead, I hadn't thought of that.

Can I say a degree of resistance is involved? And can this resistance not be contained by an appropriate classification? Scattered throughout are forms of aside, the interjecting words of another.

Complete, with stratospheric brass, when he becomes acutely aware of his own mortality, and simply wants to leave.

Composition is one continuous accident, a rumoured presence; none of this really concerns fiction, the dregs of the novel. Call down fire.

Did anything else survive?

—Bells tolling in the distance, seditious murmur in the head, passers-by morphing into demons.

Of disconcertment: once the reader accepts the lack of orientation, she becomes oriented. (Does this mean there's no conclusion?)

Don't forget remarks on colour.

Eavesdroppage: a sudden clattering noise from the kitchen, or other peoples' mouth. Every book I've read was made of fragments. Every detail is supplanted – an experience in which even the recent past is constantly being used up, traded in.

If one writer speaks of a desert (say, of eremitism) this will conjure a quite particular image and sequence of words – a simultaneous forgetting and remembering, scratching down impressions at hazard. In this manner, letters are regrouped according to the exegencies of the case. But the stranger I met on the train had never heard of the man without qualities.

This is no more than how things are. At first, this can be unsettling, yet therein lies an abundance, an inexhaustibility; uneasiness becomes adopted sinew.

Fracture has to be addressed at some point, the gaps in between.

Genres – well, what can one say? Given the evasion of linearity and plot, how may we perceive any relationships? I am utterly lacking in imagination, can only build with what I find about me in the world. Gold I have glimpsed.

Hard copy drafts must be read aloud from the music stand. He also says that the writing is an elaborate analogue simulation. (Not sure about this, but yes: steampunk interiors.)

Now he is washing his hands at the rusty tap.

He then observed that the parenthesized comments act in counterpoint to gravity. He wakes up back in an operating room close to the front, grey dawn seeping through the skylight.

Hey, in Einstein's doctrine, the well-specified instant remains an absolute! Honesty doesn't come into it. (How about, 'What I'm Not Doing'?) Another says writing can be made in small steps, purged of self-loathing.

I appreciate the use of quixotic. I began to make a list of writers who are important to me – any excuse for a list – then felt a resistance to including it. I began with an unfathomable attraction to certain words, allowing them to leach into their surroundings as they deemed fit. I began with material culled from notebooks, carried always, gradually expanding this material over time. I began writing the portraits of anyone and everyone. It brought in little money. I called out to the angelic host.

I feel this covers just about everything I can think of. I can convince myself that the act of writing responds to an unconscious hunger, a definition of the book as living talisman. Several times I've found myself looking up various obscure flowers; I can't think of any more to say. At first, I didn't believe that I could do this, then I accepted that I could. You see, I'd like to feel that something universal and everyday is being invoked, which could turn a nerve in anyone. I think of the book as hermetic. I struggle to identify metaphor; things are what they are. I cannot recognize. If there is a book, I can't see it. I once dreamt I wrote one that was composed entirely of invented words. (If so, what's the significance of this?) I've never done this before, sat with my back to the entrance, writing as if my life depended on it.

Imagine photographing writing. (No.) I'm composing this in the laundromat, face-to-face with a tumbler. I'm not integrated; I'm not sure I know what a naturalistic novel is. I've yet to unearth a narrative in my own or any of the lives I've collided with. I'm reluctant to credit one writer before another. I'm tempted to list science fiction, crime, horror and the supernatural, comedy, mediaeval romance, holy writ, the historical novel, and miscellaneous warfares. I'm trying to think *around* myself. I kept writing and could not stop. In the absence of any overarching plot, I split into a series of compartments: a pitted cellular pattern, a mass of cavities gleaned from corrosion. It's about investigating the neutral axis.

Is that a description you'd endorse, or at least accept? Is there something about the novel that you're drawn to, in spite of the drastic contrast?

In this way they talked and I listened: '*That* one,' they said, and suddenly I knew what they were.

Fragment as evaporate.
Fragment as tesserae – wood or bone or password: a die.

I think of composition as something along the lines of 'note to self'. It might be more pertinent to say that the material drawn from memory is inenarrable. It's all a bit off-planet.

That's an interesting question, regarding conception; writing seems to have no boundaries, yet everything is weighed at anchor. Writing can work directly on the nervous system, bypassing interpretation.

It's said that writing often happens on trains. The pursuit is an attempt to draw structures from an existence that seem more resonant than those inherited, and invariably struggled against. It would be unhelpful to read while expecting events to connect with one another. I used to be irrepressible.

Let it be clear that this is not a matter of idle games of calculation. Fragmentation in the act of reading forms a much-needed symmetry.

Many are the *non sequiturs* that have little or no obvious link to their surroundings.

'Maybe,' he thought, 'I've been living here alone too long. I've become strange.'

But he could not leave, as this felt like returning to somewhere that did not need returning to.

'Maybe I'm reading things in the wrong way, in the wrong order. Maybe it's my head or my eye or my tongue, drifting as one continuous thought, silenced only by chapter headings in the broken passage of time. My vision, it was odd that day, had become *corrugated*.'

A translucent halo of liquid flame forms about his head.

I think of this as a species of writing that is concrete. No age has been so self-conscious.

Note to self: get a proper job. Notwithstanding, the writing does contain narrative strands, tributaries.

Of love and of contact with other worlds; all writing is prayer. Of throwing something *ahead of oneself*. A correspondence that occurs to me is with the programmatic secrecy of the heretics: Gnostics, Cathars, acolytes of Mani (only ex-create et cetera). Or an editor's annotated remarks to herself while trawling through a manuscript. Should I be looking elsewhere for a context, maybe something that transgresses the novel altogether? Perhaps rising plainchant, recusant gospel: pain soup.

Personally, I read this motif in relation to the act of giving flowers to the dead. There's something egalitarian about the fragment.

> Picture the construction of a gothic cathedral without a ground-plan, clusters of teeming detail from the outset. There's no plot, although a great many things happen. It comes out of nothing and returns: perfect grace.

Or,

> Picture the making of a mosaic without the guidance of an overview, its maker navigating the placement of each fraction by chance, face pressed close to the frozen pavement.

A piece broken off, the underfinished portion: I am, I remember, I watch, and although there are no voices. . . .

Play.

Poet equals maker, more or less. (Could someone check this, please?)

A protozoan of ever-changing shape: any attempt to forget – the positioning of choirs in separate places, to sing in countrapuntal mass.

Rare or archaic words often stand in for neologisms, by accident as it were, an undercover obscurity. The recollections interwoven throughout are deeply embedded; they remain anonymous, untraceable for the reader (unless one happened to be a witness, and furthermore could remember). Right now, of course, everything is out of the question.

Roots include anecdotal detail, mangled dictionary definitions and unacknowledged, often skewed and deeply interred citations, or citations grafted together to form hybrids – to wit, 'The death from which you shrink is sure to overthrow you'.

See notes on colour, for example, the colours of misremembered films. See notes on weaving.

Shadow of a fragment, a time and space intermediate, something given. Fragment as cherished gift.

Or simply attempting to write down everything you've ever noticed happening (in that sense, the task is straightforward enough). Someone once said reading your fiction is like landing in an unknown country – there are familiar markers but the terrain is always new. I am aphrodisiac for you, and vice versa.

Someone once said reading your work is like being drawn into endless, superbly crafted cul-de-sacs, yet always being able to find one's way home.

Then, something about masters and slaves and whether it is ever possible for them to become brothers in spirit.

'So now for the rest of your life, you are cast out *here*,' she says, gesturing toward a nearby wasteland.

Some of these routines contain attempts at humour, others quarantined irony. Suppose the content were merely a series of questions endlessly repeated, after all? I can't jettison this approach, cannot casually shift my attention to another mode.

Thank you, I knew I'd end up quoting myself. We took the decision to modify the small number of dating errors that appear, a history of ruptures. I have failed.

The abandonment of time is disconcerting, yet seems to function. I just kept wishing he'd get on with the story, yet felt madly goaded to write myself. (Try reading the chapters either side.) The circumstances in which I undertook this are those of a common existence: the fading hallucination and other media.

Consider the impossibility of truly sharing a single memory with another human being.

Then she says, 'The approach is aleatory.'

To which he replies, 'As with all forms of divination, I have no idea of the outcome, nor would I ever wish to, having no desire to know anything. Once the result becomes apparent, I still don't know what's happened, what has been summoned.'

One day I watched someone knitting on a train and realized this was nothing like writing.

The novel can't exist because it is so readily interrupted, ever-prepared for its own discontinuity: a sum of retrievals. The point is that such writing, by its very nature, resists any given genre – but we all know that words have the power to shapeshift us.

The reader will find numerous references to Hermes. There are references to mineralogy, human anatomy, the periodic table, meteorology, alchemy, botany et cetera. Sequences are repeated; I relish tasks that appear mindlessly systematic. But there will always be some detail that doesn't fit.

Herein is an autonomy – numberless contradictions, a resistance to equilibrium. There's much dream-work. There is sustenance in the fragment.

Nothing very much remains to be said. There were impenetrable marshes on the steppe. (How do you know all this?) The scale is one of several features that seem to bring the book into collision with the centuries. Readings aloud are multiple, and doubtless way beyond what other writers might consider a tolerably sane practice. The text is built.

I can only begin to list. The text often reads as self-reflexive instruction. A triptych must balance, peak at a zigzag centre. Just then someone rang me up to find out whether I'd ever been an accident.

The uncertain direction makes extrapolating personal references a challenge; a world must be apprehended rather than comprehended. Writing refuses to be corralled into any existing or undiscovered category – it changes direction quite suddenly, veers off at a tangent. An author could be a distant relative of trauma.

Fuck, this bewildering and endless task of marshalling.

This is impertinent, perhaps. I'm intrigued by the circumstances in which someone would undertake such a visionary and unworkable vocation.

The task is impossible, of course, but I feel driven to make the attempt, the interweft of untold fictions. Here are some common concerns: defamiliarization, allusive citation, words thieved (if that's possible), found language, the emptying of ashes into the sea.

Fantasize a final endpoint, a time when there's nothing left to write.

> To make his voice as clear as possible for the decisive conversation that was now imminent he coughed a little, as quietly as he could, of course, since this noise too might not sound like a human cough for all he was able to judge.

To place a detail amid other details – encircling, navigating one another. This repeated action tore every scrap of skin off the back of my hands.

Watch out, this is the edge. (Wouldn't it be easier if we just met?)

All the time we have bodies it will be impossible to meet face-to-face. There's rumour abroad that we know a great deal about ourselves, but what remains unwritten seems important too, the invisible foil illuminating a residue.

So, to conclude, I find myself trying to frame analogies with other things I'm vaguely aware of. I had some questions.
In the next room meanwhile there was complete silence.

He was puzzled; everything about her puzzled him. Spores were implanted to see how and what they might germinate. Writing makes itself. (Yes, we know.)

You, either.
I mean your tendency to crook language flexed into a curve, a curve of forgetting.

This composition was written in response to the editors' enquiry about the author's method of composition.

In Transit (Christine's House)[1]

Ken Edwards

But the light was creeping up and I persistently swallowed it. Having come in through my gummy eyelids, it then got up my nose.[2] Light and silence. I was on my back. It came up the stairs, emerging out of the absolute dark but the stairs didn't creak. It got in my face.[3]

    We have to get out of here, I said.

    But nobody moved.

---

[1]Ed: Nice contrast to the other submissions, thank you for offering it!
KE: Thanks for the appreciation. However, I have already rejected some of these proposed amendments, so I am puzzled as to why you are proposing them again. Also, you seem to have dropped a few amendments that I did accept. The piece is made out of the recycled vocabulary of the first page of CBR's *Such*, which may account for some of the eccentricities, but in any case much of the flavour, rhythm and humour will be lost if the language is normalised to this extent

[2]Ed: suggest entered or went (from 'come in'). Since the light has already entered through the eyelids, the tense logic renders 'then' obsolete. Is the intent with 'got up' to say the light irritated the nose?
KE: yes, the ambiguity is intended so leave as is
Ed: What is the ambiguity intended here, as none seems to exist. The text is quite explicit.

[3]Ed: Having already described the light being swallowed, going through eyelids, and entering the nose, why the repetition here?
KE: "got in my face" same ambiguity
Ed: Little confused about what is meant by the ambiguity. The text doesn't seem to be ambiguous. It's rather the description not moving sequentially - suggestion is to follow the light as it moves over the face.

There's a kind of atmosphere.[4] I mean, oppressive. Voices hang. One of them says these are the end times. But they[5] are the beginning times too, and the middle times, for that matter. There's a distort[6] that's upsetting; everything's got kind of mixed and slightly out of sequence, though it could be levelling out. You never know.

Today's the day, you reminded me, as if I wasn't aware,[7] that we move into Christine's house. Soon it will be our house.

My, my. Don't exaggerate.

Yes, well.

This is a time of unreality.[8] Packing started on Thursday afternoon, when Jarvis delivered the boxes. There they are, look like coffins.[9] There's a mystery to be solved.[10] Layers of it. The light waves were travelling for billions of years before they hit the stairs and started to climb. They had lost a lot of definition by then.[11] Perhaps that's why there were no creaks? It's an open and shut case. The rooms were now empty and huge. We only have evidence for[12] life in one solar system. The neighbours were divided on the question – of our departure, that is. One of them says one thing, and another another. Down the stairs. You examined your nails – perhaps you were feeling some emotion about what had gone, and what was to come. Even though there is no back-story, and there will be no closure.

So the car had been ordered, to take us to the coast. The coffins were to travel separately by van, and by way of the industrial storage units. The driver was a Turk. He spent most of the journey trying to persuade us not to take our holidays in Greece, despite the current economic advantages of doing so, but as I was mostly on the phone on the back seat throughout the trip I didn't follow the meridians of his argument. All I know is that we could scent the

---

[4]Ed: Consider: A kind of atmosphere. Oppressive. Voices hang.....

[5]Ed: suggest: these

[6]Ed: suggest: An upsetting distortion; everything's mixed.... is there a reason for using the verb as a noun? it isn't listed in any of the standard dictionaries.

[7]Ed: consider inserting: already

[8]Ed: consider: The time of...

[9]Ed: consider: boxes, looking like....

[10]Ed: consider: A mystery.....

[11]Ed: consider: climb, having lost a lot of definition.

[12]Ed: of ... or: for the existence of life
KE: yes, "of" for "for"

coast even before it swung into sight,[13] and felt the atmosphere lift before the light did.

When we arrived, we found the van had preceded us. It was parked between the house and the pub, outside which[14] people, perhaps local punters, smoked. But Christine had not vacated the premises, so it was a stalemate.[15] The notice says the house must be vacated. Her people were still carrying out manoeuvres. Not to mention furniture. We paid off[16] the driver and retreated to Latham's Brasserie to order coffee, hang about and wait. The sun came out, and there are charming walks to be had here. We saw all this through the restaurant window. But that's for later. We never saw her. Dust accumulated for four and a half billion years. Then[17] the phone rang.

The young man had evidently been drinking all day at the table in front of the pub next door, and now he had a grievance: the van, parked in front, was blocking his view. Of the sea, he said. But the sea is not visible from here in any case; at most, a glimpse. That's what the agent had told us, a sea glimpse. Never mind. So he tried to haul himself up into the cab of the van; however, he was too far gone to accomplish the move. The men stared in disbelief, and some amusement, as they came and went. In one hand, he clutched a bottle of wine, which he refused to relinquish. His eyes moved in their orbits. There are five moons, five planets on his Hawaiian shirt, and fresh stains on his shorts. He had to admit defeat on this one. But he was formidable, he brooked no opposition. His demeanour grave, he entered the open double-leaved front door before we could stop him, went through it and between and stood in the airy hallway, swaying gently. It was a natural opening. As if nobody had ever accused him of going too far. Nice house, he said, I remember it well. From my childhood. He added suddenly: I should like to lie down now.
> Do you know Christine? you inquired.
> Who?

---

[13]Ed: consider: before seeing it,

[14]Ed: outside of which

[15]Ed: consider moving this phrase to continue from the next sentence: the premises. The notices says the....vacated, so it was a stalemate.

[16]Ed: del

[17]Ed: del

I mean the owner of the house.

I cannot say.

He is, possibly, insouciant. He sits abruptly down on a chest that you might have thought placed there for that purpose and not in the random position it had actually arrived at[18] – such is his authority – places the bottle on the floorboards and takes out from his pocket[19] a fag he has previously (when sober?) rolled. Sits as though reading an invisible book.

You can't smoke here, I said

Do you mean I may not?

We have to draw the line somewhere. This is our house.

I thought you said it was Christine's house.

He rose, bowed politely, held in the air the roll-up for everyone to see, like a conjuror about to perform a trick, and then[20] swiftly hid it in the lapel pocket of his shirt.

I can, but I shall not. He spoke magnificently.

He bowed, at least we thought he was bowing, head down, but no, he's picking up the wine bottle. This one has a special quality, he said, would you like some?

We have no glasses, I explained, they've not yet been unpacked.

Never mind. He salutes us. The bottle rides high as he gulps avidly, and is drained. I imagine that he is toasting the new occupation. Did you know, he said anxiously, wanting to make further conversation, did you know the transit of Venus occurs today? It will not re-occur – is that a word? – it will not re-occur, he said, for another one hundred and five years.

George? The heavy woman appeared in the doorway, blocking the light. More like an eclipse than a transit. George, come out of there.

With her towering status, her voluminous skirt, she looks like she is capable of kicking him in the buttocks.

The young man's hair is more tousled, it is actually pronged, he is someone who creaks.

And she said: George, let's go, this house isn't yours, it

---

[18]Ed: consider deleting and replace: randomly--

[19]Ed: consider: and places...., taking from....
KE: OK, I'll go for this one

[20]Ed: del

belongs to these people.

No, it doesn't, he said, apparently it belongs to Christine.

It's our house as of now. I don't know precisely when the transit happened. Silence collects. The five moons unless planets move and the orbits surround the silences. But the house has no moons. Beneath the bland carapace of its atmosphere it is terrestrial, rocky, volcanic, toxic. The transit takes place when the house passes directly in between the sun and earth, becoming visible against the solar disc. The disc may be projected onto a white sheet of paper, where the slow travel of the smaller disc may safely be observed. More like ellipses than eclipses. This happens every 243 years as a rule. That's how long the house has been here. After this period, we have returned to very nearly the same spot. Or is it? Here, the stairs don't creak, or something creaks but we don't notice. But every day, coincidentally, lasts 243 days here. We return to and have started to inhabit the house, but do we own it? How can we? There's a kind of atmosphere.[21] I mean, carbon dioxide and nitrogen, with clouds of sulphuric acid. The house's rotation is retrograde, that is to say[22] the sun rises to the west of it and sets in the east. The house is a cage of wood, clad in brick and more cladding, full of things, creaking in the full force of high winds. Hit the side of it with a hammer, dissect it, whatever, it will still be there. It belongs to whoever is in it and to nobody.

The next transit will be on 10–11 December 2117. We look forward to it.[23]

---

[21] Ed: del ... A kind of atmosphere, carbon....

[22] Ed: consider deleting

[23] Ed: Last two paragraphs are gems! A very unusual piece, quietly humorous, would make a very welcome addition to the Festschrift.

FOOTNOTE TO THE FOOTNOTES: This vampiric piece, using up all the words on the first page of her novel *Such* (1966), was originally submitted for a proposed festschrift for the late Christine Brooke-Rose, British novelist and scholar, who was herself a practitioner of Oulipian constraints. After irreconcilable differences ensued between one of the editors (Ed) and myself (KE) the piece was withdrawn from publication.

Donald Revell's Reinvention of Memoir as an Act of Faith

Norman Weinstein

One of the pleasures of teaching writing in community settings removed from Academia is freedom. The typical English department genre courses in which various forms of fiction and non-fiction are presented as fait accompli can become re-configured into fluid quests to get to the bottom of what genres can become rather than conventional rehashes of what genres have been. One particularly satisfying course I offered at a community literary center was a memoir class using Dante's *La Vita Nuova* (in Mark Musa's translation) as the sole required text. One student found Dante unreadable even in Musa's lucid English, and complained that he signed up for this course in order to write a memoir that was, as he put it, "100% myself." Surely Dante couldn't help him with that goal – or could he? Without interjecting my own discomfort with the mass popularity in recent decades of memoirs as exercises in capriciously narcissistic confessions cohered by pop psychological clichés, I invited my student to think of his life as an allegory, something more than "100% myself," a thought likely triggered in equal measure by John Keats and Charles Olson. He didn't go for it – but others in the class did. And how I wish now that Donald Revell's *Essay: A Critical Memoir* I could have had in hand at that moment.

In addition to Dante's, other reformulations of memoir did came to mind:: spiritual memoirs of Saints Augustine, Theresa, and John of the Cross, the hybrid mix of memoir/day book in haiku and prose by Basho and Issa, and in our time, Robert Duncan's H.D. Book and "Truth and Life of Myth."

Revell's *Essay: A Critical Memoir* reflects lessons learned from these sources – and something more. He limits the scope of his memoir to an inspired/inspiring time and locale: New York in the late 1960s. And focuses upon a constellation of people and events related to the anti-war movement during the Vietnam War. Partitioning his personal memory in this fashion during an era of extraordinary personal and national turbulence sets the stage for allegorical presentation: the stark confrontations of the powers behind the State and Army contrasted with the anarchistic bands of the Army Against the Army.

All of the makings of a disastrous literary production Revell had at his fingertips. His focus easily could have descended into a simplistically stereotypic anti-war tract replete with expected rounds of self-righteous rage. And given Revell's devotion to Christianity, his memoir might have been variations on a theme by Daniel Berrigan or Thomas Merton: prophetic denunciation of a nation's bloodthirsty Imperial will leavened with lyrical poetic embellishments rooted in prophetic books of the King James Bible.

But Revell saves himself, and us, from that predictable an outcome by realizing, as my former student could not, by taking Dante on as a "Virgil" guiding him through dark memory corridors, so he could become an astute chronicler of more than "100% myself." One obvious guide Revell could have joined company with in this memoir venture would have been Rimbaud, particularly since Revell's notable Rimbaud translations gave him a possibility of a nourishing alliance in poetic imagination. A Rimbaud connection could have taken as a starting point Rimbaud's creed so often mined by the American avant-garde: "I is the other."

But Dante served Revell as a faith advisor, deeply seated in Christian theological imagination, while Rimbaud was faithless, save for that tragic yearning for an eternal Christmas.

Also Revell's choice of Dante as literary companion and memoir-shaper brought into focus a key theme Rimbaud couldn't illuminate for him: the dynamics of devotion to an archetypal female muse. In an astonishingly polyphonic, associatively dense opening section of *Essay*, Revell writes:

> BEING A LIFE, the new life has its passages – from
> danger to rescue, from beasts to abandonment
> to shepherded festal days. They become cosmic
> sometimes: Dante awakens from a dream of Beatrice to
> eternal Beatrice, finding himself harried in the dark wood
> by three fierce creatures. Then he goes off across the
> universe.

As Revell's memoir evolves, different manifestations of faces of eternal Beatrice arise: from a grade school teacher's maternal loveliness in introducing to him the spirit-life of great poetry, to Revell's sister Roberta who like Beatrice suffered death tragically all too soon, and finally to Sylvia, a Beloved shedding light on how to read the allegorical dimensions of Revell's New York life thick in the anti-war movement of 1968:

> Sylvia, an Arcadian by name, was the friend of some
> friends of mine. One afternoon I saw her fall and tear the
> seat of her dungarees. The gesture, the nonchalance (to
> use Whitman's word) with which she folded the rough
> tear together and went on speaking to her friends, was
> unspeakably lovely. I'm saying nothing about symbols.
> This is allegory. I fell in love, and never spoke to her until
> an accident of the anti-war movement made a change.

The allegory that Revell insists upon – another defiance of convention literary practice – is not the arduous trek dramatized by Dante in the *Commedia*, or even the multiple voluptuous pleasures of a life hitchhiking on the open road. For Revell, memoir finds its stage set in pageants, replete with passionate dances, and pageants serve as occasions to reconstitute memory with unfailing accuracy:

> Our lives are loves, surely. But comes a time we
> must love rightly. Else we risk the oblivion of love,
> disappearing back to Limbo. Surely our loves appear in
> perfect order, in poetry, in pageant.

This sense of memoir as allegory actualized in pageant Revell distills from Shakespearian pageants in *The Winter's Tale* and *The Tempest*. But there might be a non-literary inspiration only hinted at in Revell's accounts of his life in the anti-war movement of 1968. As one who was there in the midst of these events in New York, I can easily view those anti-war events as pageants in the service of radically interrupting the usual narratives of everyday American life as it was supposed to be for Middle and Upper classes. In David Antin's phrase, these frequent 1968 demonstrations came to be perceived by the Body Politic as "a screw in a shoe," a persistent irritant throwing into frequent disequilibrium the American Capitalist Dream Machine. But more than irritant, these anti-war pageants were transformational psychological and spiritual and aesthetic rites of passage for those of us blessed/cursed to be young then. As William Blake felt the specific and terrifying weight of the word "war" as he composed his prophetic poems, so we in 1968 participated in an allegory of our time where "war" was a word wandering through fields of lines of poetry only to find solace in the company of the word "Eros" and then accompanied by the word "Psyche" in a myth that has life only when set in motion in choreographed pageant.

After viewing a life creating groundbreaking art as principled resistance to life-denying values, what then? One possibility, and far from the only possibility, is participating in thoroughgoing life of writing as non-stop spiritual practice. This avenue was opened interestingly for even the most spiritually skeptical among us through Jerome Rothenberg's fertile sense of poets as technicians of the Sacred. And while I'm tempted to read Revell's memoir through that lens, there is something about Revell's Christian devotion as reflected throughout his oeuvre that makes him for me less a technician of the sacred than translator of the sacred. Rothenberg's category proved immensely inviting to a spectrum of contemporary American poets with proclivities toward making sacred their private orgiastic ecstasies (Clayton Eshleman, Michael McClure, and Allen Ginsberg could easily share uneasy companionship on such a phallicly masted lifeboat). But Revell is actually a rara avis: a mainstream Christian writer deeply practicing Modernism. In fact, he may be one of a handful of poets of our era (Fanny Howe would be another) who translates a strong tributary of liberal Christian theology into first-order revolutionary lyrical poetry.

This slim and potent book was published with the exquisite care I've come to expect from Omnidawn, a Press that arguably has done the most to carry on the tradition of poetry publishing sustained by John Martin's Black Sparrow Press. The cover art consists of one of William Blake's illustrations to Dante, of Beatrice addressing Dante. Revell's artful memoir is fully worthy of that illustration, and makes Blake's reading of Dante that much richer by contextualizing Dante and Blake in an eternal 1968 cry to end inner and outer war.

Donald Revell, Essay: A Critical Memoir, *Omnidawn (Oakland, CA, 2015), $17.95*

A Glorious Thought Excursion

Steve Potter

John Olson's thoughtful and often humorous new novel, *In Advance of the Broken Justy*, opens with a somewhat Kafkaesque quest to find medical attention for the narrator's wife's infected eye late at night in Paris during a doctor's strike and ends on January 8th, 2015 with news of the previous day's terrorist attack on the Charlie Hebdo offices playing on the television in their hotel room as they prepare to leave for home.

In the pages between the personal crisis and the international one, we are introduced to the oddball mix of neighbors in the narrator's thin-walled building who are driving him and his wife, Ronnie, crazy with noise from construction projects, stomping feet, and rather explicitly audible sounds of digestive functions from a neighboring bathroom. Noisy neighbors are enough to drive any introverted, bookish homebody nuts, but our unnamed protagonist tells us, during a seemingly obsessive and often hilariously aggrieved section of narration reminiscent of Thomas Bernhard, that he additionally suffers from hyperacusia — a heightened sensitivity to noise, and tinnitus — ringing in the ears, as well as Generalized Anxiety Disorder for which he has been prescribed a variety of antidepressants through the years.

It's not only their immediate living situation that is cause for aggravation, the couple are also dealing more generally with a growing dissatisfaction with life in rapidly-changing Seattle. Olson writes that his dislike of Seattle, "evolved over a period of time, like an allergy that starts out with a minor rash and then grows into strange secretions and the constant application of topical ointments." As their disaffection with Seattle grows, so does their love of Paris. "...we each felt an attachment that had become deeply emotional, like a drug. We had become addicted to this city. It inhabited us, as Ronnie put it."

The love of Paris among certain artistically-inclined Americans has a longstanding literary and cinematic history, of course. Mr. Olson's novel continues a lineage tracing back at least as far as Ernest Hemingway's *A Movable Feast* and F. Scott Fitzgerald's "Babylon Revisited" through Richard Yates's *Revolutionary Road* to Woody Allen's *Midnight in Paris*. Unlike Gil Pender, the protagonist of Mr. Allen's film, who is mostly enthralled with fantasies of Cole Porter, Hemingway, the Fitzgeralds, Gertrude Stein and other American ex-pats in Paris during the Jazz Age, Olson's two protagonists are most interested in actual French poets, writers and artists such as; Rimbaud, Georges Perec, Michel Tournier, Gaston Bachelard, Raymond Queneau and Pierre Michon. And while their yearning for Paris is similar to that of the couple at the center of *Revolutionary Road*, it is a rather more grown-up and grounded love of the City of Lights. Olson's protagonists are a pair of older, working-class poets not young, upper-middle-class, suburban dilettantes like Yates's Frank and April Wheeler.

In addition to their dissatisfaction with home and city, the couple are also dealing with the loss of their beloved car, the broken Subaru Justy of the novel's title. After attempting to adapt to a car-less life, including several comic misadventures with public transit and Car2Go, the narrator takes some money out of savings to buy another used Subaru but somewhat spontaneously decides he'd rather take a trip to Paris than own a car again. Ronnie agrees. Plans are made, tickets are purchased, and their ongoing study of French is kicked into a higher gear. Away they go.

The narrator alludes to dark and outrageous moments in his past, back when he was still drinking and taking drugs. "At the age of eighteen, I left my father's house and struck out for California, following the scent of sex, drugs and rock 'n' roll. I was into Dylan and the Rolling Stones. I liked the Beatles, but they remained a bit too wholesome for my rebel-without-a-cause setup. And after reading Aldous Huxley's seminal essay, *The Doors of Perception*, I had a raging desire to experiment with psychedelic drugs."

He tells briefly of getting beaten up at a New Years Eve party in Burien, attending Alcoholics Anonymous meetings, and three failed marriages. One suspects Olson could write some fine fiction of wild times, drunkenness, heartache and despair in a Kerouacian or Carveresque vein if he felt the urge to mine his past, but part of what I love about this novel is that it doesn't do that. The image of the artist as a young wild man is a popular one and there have certainly been more than enough misbehaving poets, musicians, painters, novelists and so forth to give that cliché some weight, but what makes an artist an artist is serious, longstanding dedication to one's art. It's refreshing to read a novel that dispenses with the youthful misbehavior in a few short sentences and instead depicts the couple at its center as actual grown-up artists.

In Advance of the Broken Justy is not a novel which glorifies the wild kicks of youth or wallows in the despair of drunkenness and divorce, but rather one which celebrates more mature, quiet kicks like the contemplation of works of art in the Musée d'Orsay, the Louvre, and the Georges Pompidou Centre. It is a celebration of bookstores not barrooms. The narrator and Ronnie go on a sort of literary safari, with guidance provided by a list of the best bookstores in Paris received via email from the French poet Claude Royet-Journoud, and enjoy a cafe visit with the poet and translator Michel Deguy.

"One of the main reasons I wanted to go to Paris was so I could stand in a real bookstore once again before I die," Olson writes. "The bookstores in the United States have deteriorated into something little better than a gift shop, or those book and magazine shops you sometimes see at the airport. Trashy titles. Nothing of any real interest." He's not grown so jaded that he's lost all perspective, however, and can still see quality on those rare occasions it may be found. He goes on later in that passage to praise Elliott Bay Books and Open Books and elsewhere declares Magus Books in the University District to be one of the best, if not *the* best, used bookstores he's ever been to.

While at certain points it's clear that the author's imagination is at play, much of *In Advance of the Broken Justy* reads close to straight autobiography. That, of course, does not necessarily mean that it is, but the pleasures of reading the novel, for me, were often more akin to those of nonfiction. David Shields, among others, would argue that the distinction between fiction and nonfiction is meaningless. Whiile there is some validity to that stance in that in either case the author is working with a blend of memory and imagination, I think it is a bit of an overstatement. Phillip Lopate writes in a section of *To Show and To Tell: The Craft of Literary Nonfiction* in which he compares and contrasts the tendencies of nonfiction versus those of fiction that, "What makes me want to keep reading a nonfiction text is the encounter with a surprising, well-stocked mind as it takes on the challenge of the next sentence, paragraph, and thematic problem it has set for itself.... None of these examples read like short stories or screenplays; they read like what they are: glorious thought excursions."

It is Olson's surprising, well-stocked mind which is of the greatest interest here, the consciousness which regards what happens more so than the particulars of what happens, that takes interesting digressions into considerations of the work of Bob Dylan, Marcel Duchamp, Georges Braque, and organic chemist August Kekulé among others. Of the other books I've read recently, it is Patti Smith's second memoir, *M Train*, I find it most similar to in both tone and content. Smith, the poet-rocker legend, and Olson, the poet's poet who can count luminaries such as Michael McClure, Clayton Eshleman and the late, great Philip Lamantia among his fans, are exact contemporaries, Ms. Smith being the elder by only a matter of months. Their influences overlap to a considerable degree. Both books weave together narratives of domesticity and travel. Both books present the day-to-day lives of practicing artists and consider the lives of their artistic influences. Both books recount journeys to literary sacred ground in search of a sort of spiritual contact high with forebears and idols.

Mr. Lopate's phrase, "glorious thought excursions," seems like the perfect description of much of Olson's output. Fans of his prose poetry will find moments replete with the reeling riffs of surrealistic, hallucinatory lyricism familiar from his books such as *Oxbow Kazoo, Echo Regime, Logo Lagoon* and *Eggs & Mirrors* in the pages of *In Advance of the Broken Justy.* Preparations for the sale of their 500 square foot condo and a move away from their infuriatingly noisy building (preparations for naught, as it turns out, for neither sale nor move ever transpire within the pages of the novel) instigates a stream of thoughts on the nature of reality leading eventually to the following passage:

> When consciousness meets reality the result is milk. Traffic lights blossom into prayer wheels. Laundry folds itself into armies of tide pool angst and marches around like generalities of floral chambray. Rain falls up instead of down. The acceptance of frogs liberates bubbles of pulp. Time sags with basement ping pong tournaments. Garrets ovulate glass bagatelles. Realism percolates prizefight sweat. Details sparkle like crawling kingsnakes in the mouth of a Mississippi attorney.

In Advance of the Broken Justy is a thoughtful, grown-up novel for the sort of thoughtful, grown-up readers who seek out real bookstores and is not likely to have much appeal to fans of those trashy, escapist titles found in the sad, little book and magazine shops in airports Olson derides.

John Olson, In Advance of the Broken Justy, *Quale Press,* www.quale.com, *2016*

Notes on Contributors

Eleanor Antin works in photography, video, film, installation, performance, drawing and writing. One-woman exhibitions include the Museum of Modern Art, the Whitney Museum and her retrospective at the Los Angeles County Museum of Art. As a performance artist she has appeared in venues around the world including the Venice Biennale and the Sydney Opera House.. She has written, directed and produced narrative films, among them the cult feature, "The Man Without a World", 1991, (Berlin Film Fest., U.S.A. Film Fest., Ghent Film Fest., London Jewish., San Francisco Jewish, Women in Film, etc.) She has written several books including *Conversations with Stalin* and the most recent *An Artist's Life* by Eleanora Antinova. She is represented by the Ronald Feldman Gallery in New York. She received a Lifetime Achievement Award in 2006 from the Women's Caucus of the College Art Association, AICA (International Assoc. of Art Critics) Best Show awards for 2002 and earlier in 1999, a Guggenheim Fellowship and the National Foundation for Jewish Culture Media Achievement Award. She is an emeritus Professor of Visual Arts at the University of California at San Diego.

Andrea Brady's books of poetry include *Dompteuse* (Bookthug, 2014), *Cut from the Rushes* (Reality Street, 2013), *Mutability: scripts for infancy* (Seagull, 2012), *Wildfire: A Verse Essay on Obscurity and Illumination* (Krupskaya, 2010), and *Vacation of a Lifetime* (Salt, 2001). *The Strong Room* is forthcoming from Crater Press. She is Professor of Poetry at Queen Mary University of London, where she runs the Centre for Poetry and the Archive of the Now (www.archiveofthenow.org). She is also co-publisher of Barque Press (www.barquepress.com).

Stuart Cooke is a poet and critic based on the Gold Coast, Australia, where he lectures at Griffith University. He has published books of poetry, translation and criticism. His next collection of poems, *Opera*, will be published later this year.

James Davies' works include *Plants* (Reality Street), *A Dog* (zimZalla), *Rocks* (blart), and *Acronyms* (onedit). He is currently working on a number of projects including: *stack, doing, snow, if the die rolls 5 then I stamp the date, changing piece*, and *yellow lines drawn on sheets of A4 paper and then placed in a box*. He edits the poetry press *if p then q* and co-organises The Other Room reading series and resources website in Manchester.

Rachel Blau DuPlessis. The work *Graphic Novella* from which these DuPlessis pages were taken has been published by Xexoxial Editions and can be ordered directly from their website <http://Xexoxial.org/is/graphic_novella/by/rachel_blau_duplessis> . She is the author of *Drafts*, a long poem written from 1986 to 2012 and published by Salt Publishing and Wesleyan University Press. Book-length selections of *Drafts* appear in French and Italian, and poems in Flemish and Spanish. Her recent books—both poetry and poetry with collage--are *Interstices* (Subpress, 2014) and *Graphic Novella* (Xexoxial Editions, 2015). Forthcoming are a chapbook called *POESIS* from Little Red Leaves, the books *Eurydics* from Further Other Book Works, and *Days and Works* from Ahsahta. Recent journal appearances include *Conjunctions, Cordite, Lute & Drum, ATTN, Journal of Poetics Research, VLAK, Po&Sie*, and *alligatorzine*.

Ken Edwards' books include the poetry collections *Good Science* (1992), *eight + six* (2003), *No Public Language: Selected Poems 1975-95* (2006), *Bird Migration in the 21st Century* (2006), *Songbook* (2009); the novels *Futures* (1998) and *Country Life* (2015); and the prose works *Bardo* (2011), *Down With Beauty* (2013) and *a book with no name* (forthcoming from Shearsman in 2016). He has been editor/publisher of the small press Reality Street since 1993. He lives in Hastings, on the south coast of England, where he plays bass guitar and sings with The Moors and Afrit Nebula, bands he co-founded with Elaine Edwards and others.

Norman Fischer is a poet, essayist, and Zen Buddhist priest. A graduate of the University of Iowa Writer's Workshop, his latest poetry collections are *Magnolias All At Once* (Singing Horse, 2015) *Escape This Crazy Life of Tears: Japan 2010* (Tinfish, 2014), and *The Strugglers* (Singing Horse, 2013). His latest prose works are *What Is Zen? Plain Talk for a Beginner's Mind* (Shambhala Press, 2016), and *Experience: Thinking, Writing, Language and Religion* (University of Alabama Press, 2015).

John Hall has been making poems for pages since 1966 and visual poems for over two decades. *Keepsache* is a selection designed to complement the earlier *Else Here* (Etruscan). A new collection, *As a said place*, will come out from Shearsman in 2017. In recent years he has collaborated with the late Lee Harwood, Emily Critchley, David Prior and Ian Tyson as well as with Peter Hughes. johnhallpoet.org.uk

Sarah Hayden is a European (Irish) woman whose poems have appeared in the likes of *Tripwire, Scree, Steamer, The Internal Leg and Cutlery Review* and *datableed*. Her chapbooks, *System Without Issue* (Oystercatcher Press) and *Exteroceptive* (Wild Honey Press) came out in 2013 and she now needs to make a new one. She lectures in American literature at the University of Southampton. Her monograph on Mina Loy is on the way next year from University of New Mexico Press, and she is currently writing a book, *Peter Roehr—Field Pulsations*, with Paul Hegarty. She is a co-organizer of the SoundEye Poetry Festival in Cork.

Peter Hughes runs Oystercatcher Press. His *Selected Poems* was published by Shearsman in 2013 alongside *'An intuition of the particular': some essays on the poetry of Peter Hughes*. Reality Street has published *Allotment Architecture* as well as Peter's versions of the complete sonnets of Petrarch, *Quite Frankly*. The first part of his Cavalcanti project is available from Equipage. The complete *Cavalcanty* will be out from Carcanet in 2017.

John James resides in Cambridge, England, and Puisserguier, Languedoc. His recent publications include: (2011) *In Romsey Town*, Cambridge: Equipage; (2012) *Cloud Breaking Sun*, Old Hunstanton: Oystercatcher Press; (2014) *Songs In Midwinter For Franco*, Cambridge: Equipage; (2015) *Sabots*, Hunstanton: Oystercatcher Press; and forthcoming 2016, with Bruce McLean, *On Reading J H Prynne's Sub Songs*, Ashburton: QoD Press.

Nathaniel Mackey is the author of six books of poetry, the most recent of which is *Blue Fasa* (New Directions, 2015); an ongoing prose work, *From a Broken Bottle Traces of Perfume Still Emanate*, whose fifth volume, *Late Arcade*, is forthcoming from New Directions in 2017; and two books of criticism, the most recent of which is *Paracritical Hinge: Essays, Talks, Notes, Interviews* (University of Wisconsin Press, 2005). *Strick: Song of the Andoumboulou 16-25*, a compact disc recording of poems read with musical accompaniment (Royal Hartigan, percussion; Hafez Modirzadeh, reeds and flutes), was released in 1995 by Spoken Engine Company. He is the editor of the literary magazine *Hambone* and coeditor, with Art Lange, of the anthology *Moment's Notice: Jazz in Poetry and Prose* (Coffee House Press, 1993). His awards and honors include the National Book Award for poetry (2006), the Stephen Henderson Award from the African American Literature and Culture Society (2008), a Guggenheim Fellowship (2010), the Ruth Lilly Poetry Prize from the Poetry Foundation (2014), and the Bollingen Prize for American Poetry (2015). He is the Reynolds Price Professor of English at Duke University.

Richard Makin's publications include the novels *Dwelling* (Reality Street, 2011) and *Mourning* (Equus Press, 2015). He is currently writing a fiction titled *Work.* The author lives at St Leonards on Sea on the south coast of England.

Of **Toby Olson's** ten novels, the most recent is *Tampico* (U. of Texas). His most recent book of poetry is *Darklight* (Shearsman). His new novel, *Walking*, will appear soon from Chatwin Books.

Peter Quartermain hopes to complete *Growing Dumb* before the end of the year -- he is currently working on Chapter 16 -- and enjoys sporadic breaks therefrom printing sundry items letterpress, reading sundry works by Meredith Quartermain, and trying to sort sundry infuriating computer glitches. He lives in Vancouver B.C. and thinks eighty is the new hundred-and-five.

Steve Potter's poems, stories and reviews have appeared in literary journals such as; *Arthur, Blazevox, Coe Review, Drunken Boat, Galatea Resurrects, Knock, Marginalia, Pacific Rim Review of Books, RUNES* and *3rd Bed.* He lives in Seattle.

Maurice Scully born Dublin 1952. Many books. Worked in Italy & Africa for a bit in the 80s. Spends his time between Spain & Ireland now. Most recent book: *Several Dances* (2014).

Philip Terry is currently Director of the Centre for Creative Writing at the University of Essex. His novel *tapestry* was shortlisted for the 2013 Goldsmith's Prize. *Dante's Inferno*, which relocates Dante's action to current day Essex, was published in 2014, as well as a translation of Georges Perec's *I Remember.*

Michael Upchurch grew up in England, the Netherlands and New Jersey, and has lived in Seattle since 1986. His novels include *Passive Intruder, The Flame Forest* and *Air,* and his short stories have appeared in *Moss, Conjunctions, Glimmer Train, The Seattle Review* and other periodicals. He was the staff book critic for *The Seattle Times* for ten years (1998-2008) and has written extensively about books and the arts for other publications, including *The New York Times Book Review, Chicago Tribune, Washington Post* and *The American Scholar.* He is married to film critic John Hartl. Find out more at www.michaelupchurchauthor.com.

Carol Watts's poetry includes *Occasionals* (Reality Street, 2011), *Sundog* (Veer Books, 2013) and *many weathers wildly comes* (susakpress, 2015). A collaborative collection with George Szirtes, *56*, is due shortly.

Norman Weinstein's books of poetry include *Weaving Fire From Water* (Wolf Peach Press, 2002)) and *No Wrong Notes* (Spuyten Duyvil, 2005). Also a book about Gertrude Stein and another about jazz, *A Night in Tunisia: Imaginings of Africa in Jazz* (Limelight Editions, 1992). Extensive articles about architecture published globally during last decade. Currently working on poems and essays that synthesize poetry, music,and architecture. Teaches Canadian Studies and Education at Boise State University.

Lightning Source UK Ltd.
Milton Keynes UK
UKOW05f0122240916

283658UK00002B/274/P